BEAR
BRYANT
ON
LEADERSHIP

BEAR BRYANT ON LEADERSHIP

Life Lessons from a Six-Time
National Championship Coach

PAT WILLIAMS
with TOMMY FORD

Advantage®

Published by Advantage, Charleston, South Carolina.
Member of Advantage Media Group.

ADVANTAGE is a registered trademark and the Advantage colophon is a trademark of Advantage Media Group, Inc.

Printed in the United States of America.

ISBN: 978-1-59932-210-0
LCCN: 2010914686

This publication is designed to provide accurate and authoritative information in regard to the subject matter covered. It is sold with the understanding that the publisher is not engaged in rendering legal, accounting, or other professional services. If legal advice or other expert assistance is required, the services of a competent professional person should be sought.

Advantage Media Group is proud to be a part of the Tree Neutral™ program. Tree Neutral offsets the number of trees consumed in the production and printing of this book by taking proactive steps such as planting trees in direct proportion to the number of trees used to print books. To learn more about Tree Neutral, please visit **www.treeneutral.com**. To learn more about Advantage's commitment to being a responsible steward of the environment, please visit **www.advantagefamily.com/green**

Advantage Media Group is a leading publisher of business, motivation, and self-help authors. Do you have a manuscript or book idea that you would like to have considered for publication? Please visit **www.amgbook.com** or call **1.866.775.1696**

*I dedicate this book to John Merrill, who first introduced me
to Tuscaloosa and the magic of Alabama's football heritage.*
—PAT WILLIAMS

*I dedicate this book to Robin and John Michael, who so
patiently shared me with Coach Paul "Bear" Bryant, his Seven Sides
of Leadership, and more than 200 people who knew him best.*
—TOMMY FORD

CONTENTS

CHAPTER ONE

- Focused on the Big Picture
- Fueled with Passion and Energy
- Finish/Results

CHAPTER TWO

- Believe it's Important to Communicate
- Be Verbally Precise — Clear, Concise, and Correct
- Optimism
- Motivation & Inspiration
- Public Speaker

THE SPARK THAT
LIT THIS BOOK

I had heard of Tuscaloosa, Alabama, and was always fascinated by the name as a kid growing up in Wilmington, Delaware, in the 1940s and 50s. I was a huge sports fan and would always relish the Saturday afternoon football reports. You'd get the latest news from Tuscaloosa, Alabama; I liked to even say the word "Tuscaloosa" because it kinda rolled off the tongue trippingly.

But, in all my years in college and pro sports, I had never visited Tuscaloosa. Then, about six or seven years ago, I got a call one day from a young man named John Merrill, who asked me to come to Tuscaloosa to speak to his church's "Welcome Back" day for college students. I accepted the invitation.

I flew from Orlando to Birmingham on a Saturday afternoon, met John at the airport, and we drove to Tuscaloosa. He put me up at the hotel right there on campus and my weekend in Tuscaloosa began.

The hotel where I was staying was on Bryant Drive, next to the Bryant Conference Center and the Bryant Museum, and down the street from Bryant-Denny Stadium. Everywhere I turned there was another photograph of Paul "Bear" Bryant, this legendary coach leaning against a goalpost or coaching from the sideline. Every office I was in had some sort of painting or photo of him. The hotel lobby was full of references to this coach.

And then they told me that before every football game, Coach Bryant comes up on the video screen and tells all the fans, "I ain't nothin' but a winner." I thought, "This man is still alive…he hasn't gone anywhere. I mean he is as alive today as he was when he was coaching Alabama to heights we've never seen before." I was automatically intrigued.

I asked myself, "Just who was this man? Why is he still so visible in Alabama?" My immediate reaction was "leadership." I'm intrigued with leadership, fascinated by it. I always want to learn about leaders and leadership. The seed for this book was planted on that first visit to Tuscaloosa.

I've since made other trips back to Tuscaloosa and still enjoy them. I still get that same sense of Bryant's presence, but at the end of the day, my question always remained, "What made him a great leader? More importantly, what can we learn from him? What leadership principles can we take from Coach Bryant and apply into our own lives?"

That's the spark that lit this book.

THE SEVEN SIDES OF LEADERSHIP

Leadership has become a gigantic industry unto itself in our country. Hardly a week goes by that I don't get another brochure or mailing piece about a leadership conference or seminar or retreat. And that doesn't take into account the books that are pouring out on leadership, seemingly by the day.

I think it all started in 1992 when a man named Donald T. Phillips wrote a book called *Lincoln on Leadership*. He spent years trying to get it published and the publishers told him that the problem is that there's just no place to put it in the bookstores; there's just no category on "leadership." So he was turned down many times.

Finally, the book was published and it became a huge success, and an industry was launched in the publishing world. Then a pastor on the west coast, John Maxwell, wrote a book called *The 21 Irrefutable Laws of Leadership*. It hit the *New York Times* bestseller list and the barn door was open at that point. Now, leadership books are coming out in droves.

And, many of them are built around people – many of the biblical personalities have books about them. We have David on leadership and Jesus on leadership and Moses on leadership, including one book called *Moses on Management*. And then there are the Civil War personalities – you can read about Robert E. Lee on leadership and Ulysses S. Grant on leadership, and when you get to World War II, the books are abounding – from Truman on leadership to Eisenhower on leadership

to Roosevelt, to Churchill, to General Patton, to General Marshall…
it just never ends.

And you can't be in the sports business unless you've written your
book on leadership. We have Pat Summit on leadership and Bobby
Bowden on leadership and Mike Krzyzewski on leadership and Joe
Torre and Lou Holtz and on and on and on.

But the one book that I wish had been written on leadership was
Bear Bryant on Leadership. I wish Coach Bryant had done it himself.
I wish he had sat down and fleshed out all of his leadership advice,
his counsel, and his principles that would affect leaders in every walk
of life. But unfortunately, Coach Bryant, who passed away in 1983,
never got around to doing that. He did write his memoirs, a wonderful
autobiography with the assistance of John Underwood that captures
many, many sides of Coach Bryant.

And speaking of sides of Coach Bryant, he has been written about
and studied from every possible angle. You can read books about his
training camp at Texas A&M and his first season at Alabama. Every
minute detail of this man's life has been written about in great detail,
except this book you're reading now, about Coach Bryant and what we
can learn about leadership from this man.

So after my visit to Tuscaloosa, I was determined to get to the
bottom of this, and I'm so delighted that we have finally launched the
project with Advantage Media Group. The research into this book has
been vast and in-depth. With the assistance of the Alabama Athletic
Department and my writing partner Tommy Ford, I've been able to
track down more than 200 people who knew Coach Bryant – who
played under him, who coached with him, who coached against him,
who covered him in the media, who worked with him in his office, and
even some of his family members. Through my discussions with them,
we have brought to a head all of Coach Bryant's leadership principles.

I am a fanatic on the subject of leadership. I have bought most of the leadership books over the years; as a matter of fact, I have almost 650 leadership books perched in my leadership library at home. In addition to that, I have spent 52 years at the highest level of college and professional athletics, the last 42 as an executive in the National Basketball Association.

Through this period and through all of my study, I come away convinced that to be a leader for the ages, a leader who makes an enormous impact, there are seven qualities or sides of leadership that must be in place. With all due apologies to my good friend John Maxwell and his *21 Irrefutable Laws of Leadership*, this book is designed to focus on these seven sides of leadership that I have discovered all great leaders possess... and match it up with what Coach Bryant did for almost 40 years in college football as a leader. The more I studied Bryant as a leader and the more interviews I did, the more convinced I became that he truly was a seven-sided leader.

So, as you read the reflections and the teaching points that come from all of these people who knew him well, the mission of this book is to make you a better leader. Whether you're leading in education, the military, the church, athletics, business, or the highest levels of government, this book is designed to help you discover the keys to being a seven-sided leader through the life lessons and demonstrations of legendary University of Alabama coach Paul W. "Bear" Bryant, whose memory will always be with us.

So, sit down and get ready for a life-changing read. Make sure you have a highlighter or pen, because you're going to be taking away a lot of practical, real-life, shoe leather-to-the pavement principles that will forever change your life as a leader.

Have a productive read!

PAUL W. "BEAR" BRYANT

On a late November day in 1981, when Alabama head football coach Paul W. "Bear" Bryant became the undisputed king of college football, when a victory ride on his players' shoulders was most deserved and certainly expected, the coach – in his own Bryant-esque way – diplomatically and quietly refused the offer.

"I didn't want them to (carry me off)," said Bryant, after his team's 28-17 defeat of rival Auburn, securing his spot in history as the game's winningest coach. "I oughta been the one carrying them and I would have if I'd been strong enough. I'd taken each one off, one at a time, if it'd taken until midnight."

The compliment was, without a doubt, vintage Bryant. Although intended only for that moment in time, his words may as well have been meant for *all* his former players throughout the years, whether at Maryland, Kentucky, Texas A&M, or Alabama. After all, Bryant once said, "If anything goes bad, I did it. If anything goes semi-good, we did it. If anything goes really good, then you did it. That's all it takes to get people to win football games for you."

As the most high-profile coach in college football history, win he did, a bunch of times. Over his storied 38-year head coaching career, Bryant won 323 games, lost 85, and tied 17. At his alma mater Alabama, Bryant's 232-46-9 record translates into a remarkable 82.4 percent winning record. Many of those 232 wins propelled Bryant's

Crimson Tide teams to six national championships and 13 Southeastern Conference crowns.

As celebrated as Bryant became, though, his early days in the fields of home state Arkansas were about as humble as one could have. Born September 11, 1913, in Moro Bottom on a three-square-mile plot of land shared with six other families, Bryant was the 11th of 12 children born to Ida and Monroe Bryant.

The Bryants made their living from the soils of the earth and the toils of their hands. Their daily routine was to haul their products – milk, butter, eggs, watermelons, chickens, hogs, cotton, and vegetables – seven miles to the market in Fordyce. The work was brutal and the hours were long, but in doing so, Bryant learned hard work, respect, discipline, dedication, and pride, traits he would one day teach to so many others.

Bryant and his family moved to nearby Fordyce when he was around 11 years old. Not long afterward, his first taste of Crimson Tide football came while listening to the play-by-play radio broadcast of Alabama's thrilling 20-19 victory over Washington in the 1926 Rose Bowl. "I never imagined anything could be that exciting," he recalled many years later. "I still didn't have much of an idea what football was, but after listening to that game, I had it in my mind that what I wanted to do with my life was go to Alabama and play in the Rose Bowl…."

Before Bryant could fulfill his football dreams, though, he had to first earn the nickname that would make him famous. One summer, when he was around 14, on a dare he wrestled a bear for a dollar a minute, clearly winning the match until the bear's muzzle popped off. Before he realized it, the bear had taken a chunk of skin from behind his ear. Bryant's quick exit kept him from collecting the dollar; instead, he acquired the nickname that would follow him forever.

Bryant's Fordyce High School Redbugs team, which won the Arkansas state championship in 1930, was led by a set of twins, Clark and George Jordan. Recruiters far and wide, including Alabama assistant coach Hank Crisp, came to see the Jordan boys. Although Crisp didn't sign the twins, who opted for the University of Arkansas, he reeled in a bigger catch – Paul W. "Bear" Bryant – and the rest is history.

Bryant played for Coach Frank Thomas at Alabama from 1932-35 as the "other end" to All-American Don Hutson. Following the 1934 season, his childhood dreams were realized when he played in the famed Rose Bowl, helping lead the Tide to a 29-13 rout of Stanford to secure Alabama's fourth national championship in 10 years. In less than a decade, he had gone from *listening* to the Rose Bowl to *playing* in it.

During his college days at Alabama, Bryant's leadership skills were obvious – class president (twice), varsity letter club president, and Omicron Delta Kappa leadership honorary. Equally impressive were his skills and toughness on the field. Against Tennessee in 1934, he played with a broken leg. When asked about it by a reporter following the game, Bryant sheepishly said, "It was just one little bone," to which assistant coach Red Drew retorted, "How many broken bones do you have to have to have a broken leg?"

After a four-year stint as an Alabama assistant, Bryant coached at Vanderbilt for two seasons, and then served in the U.S. Navy for three years during World War II. His celebrated coaching career started soon afterward, turning around programs at Maryland (1945), Kentucky (1946-53), and Texas A&M (1954-57). Then, "Mama" called.

"Mama," of course, was the University of Alabama, whose Crimson Tide football program, coached by J.B. "Ears" Whitworth, had reached rock bottom. Whitworth's abysmal 4-24-2 record from 1955-57 had the Alabama faithful clamoring for a winner, and by securing Bryant, they had their man. Just the switch of nicknames from an "Ears" to a "Bear" was enough to show that things would be much different around the Alabama football program.

Bryant wasted no time getting to work. Described in the 1958 Alabama football media guide as "the game's most successful rehabilitator of decrepid [sic] football machines," Bryant, in no uncertain terms, sent a clear message to his boys to shape up or ship out. Many of them wilted under the pressure and never made it through spring practice. Today, all those who quit, regret their decision.

Record-wise, it took Bryant only one season to turn things around in Tuscaloosa. Inheriting talent that had won only two games the year before, he finished with a respectable 5-4-1 in his first season.

Through rugged and disciplined teaching and motivation, Bryant needed only three more seasons to take the Crimson Tide to the top of the college football world. After marked improvement in 1959 (7-2-2) and 1960 (8-1-2), Alabama captured the 1961 college football national championship. Led by a defense that Bryant said "played like it was a sin to give up a point" and a steady, ball-hogging offense, the workman-like Tide outscored its opponents 297-25, the fewest points given up since Bryant was a sophomore on the 1933 squad. For the coach, it would be the first of six national crowns.

Through the 1960s, Bryant's wins – and championships – kept piling up. The 1964, 1965, and 1966 seasons represented the finest three-year run in Alabama football history, surpassed only a few years later by the 1977, 1978, and 1979 Tide squads. Indeed, the 1961 national championship was special and elevated Bryant to college football notoriety shared by very few. But it was the 1964, 1965, and 1966 teams that moved Bryant to the top of his game.

The 1964 and 1965 squads captured national titles, while the 1966 unit, despite finishing as the nation's only undefeated and untied team, was, as Bryant said, "done in at the ballot box" and finished third. Despite a slump late in the decade, the Tide's 90-16-4 record was college football's finest record of the 1960s.

Across the nation, the late 1960s and early 1970s were known for war protests, racial issues, and changes in moral values. Bryant weathered these storms off the field, but following another mediocre season in 1970, he couldn't weather his current offensive philosophy. "...I knew we couldn't win with what we had, doing what we were doing," a reflective Bryant would later say.

In a bold move, Bryant switched his offense to what characterized him best: back-to-the basics, physical, old-fashioned, grind-it-out football. With only four weeks practice and in a cloud of total secrecy, he installed the triple-option wishbone attack. In early September of 1971, on a Friday night in Los Angeles, the Southern California Trojans became the Tide's first victim. Alabama's 17-10 victory set the pace for an undefeated regular season.

Bryant and Alabama's success during the 1970s was staggering. With the wishbone in full throttle and the defense playing to early 1960s standards, the Tide roared to eight Southeastern Conference championships and three national titles (1973, 1978, and 1979).

Alabama's 103-16-1 record in the 1970s proved again to be the best in college football. During this time, the Crimson Tide provided 21 first-team All-Americans, 16 second-team All-Americans, 71 first-team All-SEC picks, and 28 second-team All-SEC selections.

After a 10-2 record in 1980, all attention in 1981 turned to Bryant's pursuit of Amos Alonzo Stagg's record of 314 victories. Talk of Stagg's record had actually begun three years earlier, shortly before the 1978 season, when long-time Bryant publicist Charley Thornton discovered that Bryant was only 42 wins away. Once the cat was out of the bag, Bryant said, "Well, if anybody's going to break the record, it might as well be me."

What took 57 years for Stagg to accomplish, Bryant eclipsed in only 37. Bryant's 315th win against rival Auburn remains a magical game in Crimson Tide lore.

Bryant's final Alabama squad in 1982 started the season like lions, but finished like lambs with an 8-4 mark. Following a loss to LSU, Bryant shocked everyone by stating that "some changes ought to be made at the top and I'm at the top." When asked if this meant he was considering retirement, Bryant replied, "I'll do anything it takes to get something done, to improve, to get better."

On December 15, Bryant did indeed announce his retirement after 25 glorious years at the Tide helm. His players, vowing to end the season on a positive note and send Bryant out a winner, rallied for a thrilling 21-15 victory over Illinois in the Liberty Bowl.

Twenty-seven days later, on Wednesday, January 26, 1983, at 1:30 p.m. CST at Tuscaloosa's Druid City Hospital, the winningest coach in the history of major college football was pronounced dead of a massive heart attack. The 69-year old Bryant's long running joke that he would "croak in a week" if he ever quit coaching was eerily near accurate.

Tributes for "The Coach" poured in from across the nation. President Ronald Reagan said Americans had "lost a hero who always seemed larger than life – a coach who made legends out of ordinary people." Former president Gerald Ford called Bryant a "superstar in the history of American football...his achievements have been indelibly written in the history of American sports."

Bryant's funeral, held at Tuscaloosa's First United Methodist Church on Friday morning, January 28, 1983, was short and simple with one eulogy.

Before the day had ended, hundreds of thousands of people (including all 10 SEC head coaches and many former Bryant players and coaches) attended the funeral, witnessed the three-mile long procession from Tuscaloosa to Birmingham, or attended graveside services at Birmingham's Elmwood Cemetery.

Other than for a U.S. president, never again will this nation see a funeral tribute quite like that for the man known as "Papa" to his family, "Paul" to his closest friends, "Coach" to his players and assistant coaches and the "Bear" to his millions of followers.

Nor, for that matter, will we ever see a life quite like his.

Chapter One

VISION

"Where there is no vision, the people perish..."

—Proverbs 29:18

The leadership experts today may disagree on some of the finer points of leadership, but vision is not one of them. Having vision is one quality on which they are unanimous.

Vision is a big reason why University of Alabama football is where it is today. You do not become one of the nation's top programs and 13-time national champions without vision. All the way back to 1892, when William G. Little brought this funny game to Tuscaloosa, Alabama, to the modern-day Nick Saban, who has already secured a national championship for the Crimson Tide in only three short seasons, vision is a must.

Alabama head football coach Paul "Bear" Bryant, in the most famous quarter-century stretch in college football history, might as well have had the word "VISION" plastered across his forehead in big capital letters. Bryant knew what vision was all about. He saw the future before it arrived. He saw over the horizon before others even opened their eyes. He saw the victory parades down University Boulevard already taking place. He saw the facilities already built. He even saw his teams' national championship trophies glistening in the

Paul W. Bryant Museum long before they were won and certainly long before there was ever a Bryant Museum.

We all know that someone who performs more than one task at the same time is called a multi-tasker. Well, we might call Bryant a multi-visionary, as he saw multiple visions simultaneously. Not only did he have a vision for each one of his players, game plans for upcoming opponents, and tweaks in his Xs and Os, but also for the future of the entire football program and athletic department.

Academics? He provided the best possible support program and was emphatic about all of his players graduating. Life skills? He always talked about his players representing the University with class. Media relations and sports publicity? He hired Charley Thornton and Kirk McNair, the best in the business, to get the word out. Accommodations? The original Bryant Hall was considered the finest athletic dorm in the nation, just another example of Bryant's vision and being way ahead of his time.

Of all Bryant's visionary accomplishments, though, none may be more personal and long-lasting than his late 1970s idea of creating the Bryant Scholarship, which offers financial assistance to the children of his former players who attend Alabama. More than a quarter-century since his death, Bryant's original gift just keeps on giving; to this date more than 700 children of Bryant players have attended the University of Alabama on the Bryant Scholarship. I bet if Bryant were here today, he'd rank that right up there with his six national championships.

When you are a visionary leader like Bryant, it does three things for you. First, it keeps you *focused*. Second, it keeps you *fueled*. And third, it helps you *finish*. As you will see, Bryant's vision made him a master at all three.

FOCUSED ON THE BIG PICTURE

One of the great problems in leadership is to become distracted — getting off the main highway and wandering on the rabbit trails. But when vision is so compelling in your life, you are like a racehorse in the Kentucky Derby with blinders on. You are locked and loaded; you are zoned in. Distractions will not keep you from focusing on the big picture.

Bryant was a big-picture kind of coach everywhere he went. Whether at Maryland, Texas A&M, Kentucky, or his alma mater Alabama, Bryant kept focused on the goals at hand. Mickey Herskowitz, a sportswriter who covered Bryant's career primarily during the Texas A&M years, said in his book, *The Legend of Bear Bryant*, "One thing I always loved about Coach is that he could always focus on something with both eyes and still find a third eye to be looking at himself while he was doing it."

Wow, I wish we all had a third eye. For Bryant's players, he was totally focused in an individual way — turning his boys into men and doing everything possible to help them get a good education and to one day make a difference in other people's lives. At the same time, he was focused in a corporate, team-oriented way — to win college football's national championship.

To his first freshman class at Alabama in 1958, he said this, as recalled in his autobiography, *Bear* (co-written with John Underwood):

> *In the fall....I met with just the freshmen. It was to be a regular thing from then on, those noon meetings, but that first one set the tone. I just sensed they were something special. I told them what football should mean to them, and what the program would be. Then I challenged them.*

I said, "What are you doing here?" And I waited. It was so quiet in there you could hear a pin drop. I said, "What are you doing here? Tell me why you're here. If you're not here to win the national championship, you're in the wrong place."

Then I told them what I thought it would take to do it, and they believed me. They believed every word. They believed it then, and they believed it all the way through school...

When I walked out that day, I knew we were going to win the national championship with that group. Before that, I had just talked about it, thought about it, and dreamed about it. This time, I was sure. And every time I saw them after that I felt the same way. The pride they had. They had a goal and they never lost sight of it.

Jimmy Sharpe, a member of Bryant's first freshman class and later an assistant coach at Alabama from 1963-73, was one of the privileged few to hear Bryant's challenge that day. "In that deep voice with those riveting eyes," Sharpe said, "he told us, in so many words, 'Here's the plan I have for you. I've watched you practice and I like what I see. If you do what I say and work hard, you'll be national champions in four years.' As time went on, we began to believe him. Coach was that far out front. His focus on the future was extraordinary."

Another set of ears in that room belonged to running back Billy Richardson. "In that first meeting with him," Richardson said, "Coach said we could be national champions by the time we graduated. He said, 'Work every day to get a little better. Believe in the guy next to you. Develop a oneness and you'll achieve your goals.'"

If that is not an example of being focused, then there's no such thing. Only four seasons later, Bryant's vision was realized as the Tide was crowned 1961 national champs. For those freshmen sitting in the room that day, the words "national championship" must have sounded like a foreign language. After all, Alabama's most recent national championship had been 17 years earlier, when most of these young men were still in diapers.

To Bryant, though, being proclaimed the best in the land was the culmination – for that group at least – of a four-year plan. He was focused on the prize, locked, loaded, and shooting for the stars. And for Bryant and Alabama, that was only the beginning. Talk of conference and national championships became everyday language in Tuscaloosa throughout his career. Bryant's focus at Alabama was always on being the best, from the late 1950s all the way to the early 1980s.

"Coach Bryant possessed a clear sense of the goal and never wavered from it," said Jack Smalley, Jr., a linebacker for Alabama in 1974-77. "His vision was defined very clearly — win a national championship. We didn't think about winning the first game. We wanted to win the last game and the one before it and the one before it. We worked back from our overall goal."

Teammates of Smalley's in the mid-1970s included Bob Baumhower, Marty Lyons, and Ozzie Newsome, all of whom went on to great NFL careers. Their sentiments about Bryant's vision and focus are similar.

"Coach Bryant was great at creating a vision for us to buy into," said Baumhower, an All-Pro with the Miami Dolphins. "He made being special seem achievable if you'd work toward it."

"Coach Bryant had good vision, not just as a coach but also in the game of life," said Lyons, a member of the New York Jets famed "New York Sack Exchange" in the early 1980s. "He stressed the right priorities – religion, family, education, and then winning football games. He said, 'If you keep those priorities in order, you can be very successful in life.'"

Newsome, a member of both the college and NFL halls of fame, said, "Coach Bryant was a man of vision and always stressed the importance of having a plan."

Evidence of Bryant's vision and focus was not reserved only for his players, but for opposing coaches as well. ESPN football analyst Lou Holtz, whose Arkansas squad lost to national champion Alabama in the 1980 Sugar Bowl, remarked, "Coach Bryant had a vision of where he wanted the team to go and a plan how to get there."

FUELED WITH PASSION AND ENERGY

To have vision, you must be fueled, possessing passion and energy. You must have enthusiasm for what you are doing. If a leader is not passionate, enthusiastic, and fueled with fire and energy for what he is doing, then guess what? Nobody else will be either. Being locked in to your vision creates fuel that generates enormous passion and energy.

Bryant was about as fueled as any coach could possibly be. Stories are legendary about his enthusiasm, passion, and competitiveness for the game. In the 1982 documentary *Nothin' But A Winner*, Bryant said, "Work is fun. I love to go to practice. I get a thrill…and I thank the good Lord every time I walk on the field. I get a big kick out of the games, and when the game is over, it's a big letdown."

Keep in mind that Bryant made those comments prior to his last season in a 44-year coaching career. Will you be saying something similar after 44 years in your profession? His passion was, to say the least, remarkable.

Clyde Bolton, long-time sportswriter for *The Birmingham News*, covered Bryant for many years and makes an interesting comparison between Bryant and his rival head coach, Auburn's Ralph "Shug"

Jordan. "I covered Shug Jordan and Auburn for 15 seasons and Bryant and Alabama for 22 seasons," Bolton said. "Coach Bryant and Coach Jordan were extremely different. Jordan would talk with you about many things. He was a historian. He'd go to New York City in the summer and attend Broadway shows.

"I've heard it said that the world belongs to the single-minded. That was Coach Bryant; he was obsessed with football twelve months a year. He was one of the most obsessed people in sports I ever met."

In Mickey Herskowitz's many Bryant stories through the years, Bryant's competitiveness, energy, and passion for the game was a common topic. "One day at Texas A&M," Herskowitz said, "a writer came to Bryant's office, which was nothing more than a little cubbyhole. He wanted to know what drove Coach and why he competed so intensely. Coach stumbled around for a while trying to get out an answer. Finally he blurted out, 'If you have a different colored shirt on than I do, I want to whip you!'

"Coach competed over most everything. Steadman Shealy was a strong Christian kid who was a terrific quarterback at Alabama. Steadman would pray with Coach in his office. One day as Steadman was leaving, Coach said, 'Steadman, I bet I pray more than you do.' He was competing over praying, too."

Bryant's competitive nature transcended to all University of Alabama sports. After all, not only was he the finest football coach in all the land, but he was the Tide's athletic director as well.

Jerry Pate, former Alabama All-American golfer and 1976 U.S. Open champion, found out the hard way how competitive Bryant was. "As my senior year was starting, I was coming into my own as an amateur golfer," said Pate, winner of eight PGA tournaments and two Champions Tour events. "I went to New Jersey to play in the U.S. Amateur and I got to the finals. On that last day, I looked in my locker and there was a telegram from Coach Bryant. It said, 'Hope all your putts drop. Win one for the University of Alabama.' Well, I got all excited and showed it to the press and the story went nationwide.

"I won the tournament, and the next Monday back in Tuscaloosa I was summoned to Coach Bryant's office. He told me how I had made my mama and papa proud and then he put my name up on the Coliseum marquee where it stayed all fall.

"The next spring, I was invited to play in the Masters and several other big events and I missed a ton of school," Pate continued. "When I got back from the Masters, Coach called me into his office and barked at me, 'Sit down! Let me tell you one thing – you're here to get a degree and beat the best SEC schools and win an NCAA title and not run all over the country playing for yourself.'

"Then he added, 'Football and basketball have won their championships this year and now it's up to golf.' Shortly after that, our golf team finished third in the SEC, which was high enough for us to clinch the SEC All-Sports Trophy. Then it all became clear to me. Since Coach Bryant was also the athletic director, his job was to win in all sports. That whole experience taught me a valuable lesson about having personal responsibility."

Jerry Duncan was a prime example of one of Bryant's "little guys" in the 1960s who was always out-sized, rarely out-quicked, but never out-smarted. At 5'11" and 190 pounds, Duncan, from his tackle position, became a favorite of Tide fans after catching three passes for 42 yards against Nebraska in the 1966 Orange Bowl, helping lead Alabama to the national championship. Duncan credits Bryant's passion for making the Tide a winner.

"When I entered the Alabama program as a freshman, we immediately picked up on Coach Bryant's passion and how much he loved to compete," Duncan said. "It rubbed off on us. There were no limits on meetings, film sessions, and practice time. In my five years, I never left Tuscaloosa in the summer time. All we did was work."

Neil Callaway, a mid-1970s lineman for Bryant and today among the more than 50 Bryant players or assistants to become a college head coach, was an astute observer of Bryant's passion for football. "He was quite a competitor," said Callaway, now head coach at the University of Alabama-Birmingham. "He had that fire burning and didn't want to lose at anything.

"After the 1977 season, we played Ohio State in the Sugar Bowl. The night before at the banquet, Coach Bryant spoke and did all right. He wasn't a great public speaker. The next speaker was Woody Hayes, a true orator. Coach Hayes went into military history and had those Ohio State fans up on their feet. The next morning at breakfast, Coach let us know clearly what he wanted us to do to the Ohio State team and their coach. We won the game, 35-6."

From that same Sugar Bowl game comes another story of Bryant's competitive nature. "Right after the 1977 season ended, I told Coach Bryant that I was planning to get married after the Sugar Bowl," said quarterback Jeff Rutledge. "He said, 'You're going to do *what*? Don't you know who we're playing?' I said, 'Yes sir, Ohio State.' He said, 'No, it's Woody Hayes – that's who we're playing.'

"From that game, I have a nice photo of Coach looking down at me with his arm around me. He was saying, 'A nice wedding present, isn't it, son?'"

Dwight Stephenson, an All-American Tide center in 1979, makes an interesting comparison between Bryant and Don Shula, his coach at the Miami Dolphins. "Coach Bryant and Coach Shula had a common quality," said Stephenson, a five-time All-Pro selection for the Dolphins. "It was the intensity and passion they had for every practice, every meeting, and every game."

I mentioned earlier that if a leader is not passionate, enthusiastic, and fueled with fire and energy for what he is doing, then nobody who works for him will be either. Bryant made sure his coaches and players bought in to his passion and fire. He would not have had it any other way.

"Coach Bryant understood he had to find a way to make others believe it was okay for them to have the same passion and fire he had," said Leon Ashford, a student athletic trainer in 1966-70. "He wanted you to believe it was the right thing to sacrifice, work hard, commit to the program and do all that it took to be successful. Coach made you believe it was real and not contrived. He was willing to make the same sacrifices that he was asking us to make."

FINISH/RESULTS

If you as a leader have a vision, not only are you focused and fueled, but it helps you finish. In football vernacular, finishing your vision gets you across the goal line and into the end zone.

Great finishes are scattered throughout Alabama's illustrious football history, but for Coach Bryant, perhaps the greatest on-the-field example of finishing a vision was the 1972 Alabama-Tennessee game in Knoxville. On the legendary "Third Saturday in October," third-ranked Alabama was favored to whip the 10th-ranked Volunteers, but with less than three minutes remaining, Tennessee had all the momentum and a 10-3 lead. Bryant's magic then took over as the Tide scored 14 points in a 36-second span to win, 17-10.

For Danny Ford, an assistant coach on that team, the comeback victory was vintage Bryant. "Coach had said before the game it was going to be a tight one and he was right," said Ford, an All-SEC end for Alabama in the late 1960s and later head coach of the 1981 national champion Clemson Tigers. "And furthermore, he told us that with two minutes left, we'd be down by a touchdown, but would score to tie it. Then, he said that after we got the ball back, 'On fourth down, we'll punt and all our fans will boo. But our defense will get the ball back again.'

"Sure enough, that's exactly what happened. We punted and got the ball back after a fumble and we won the game on a last-minute touchdown. It was uncanny how Coach Bryant would say things and they'd come true."

That, my friends, is one reason Bryant was such a great leader. Looking ahead and envisioning a win against Tennessee is one thing, but actually making it happen is another, especially with such odds stacked against him.

In the course of leading any endeavor, whether it is the Alabama football team against Tennessee, or a Fortune 500 company, or your church's administrative board, you're going to encounter obstacles – mountains to climb over, long stretches of desert, and bumpy valleys through which you have to traverse.

For Alabama and Bryant in the 1972 Tennessee game, the obstacles were plentiful – playing a heated rival on the road, a powerful wishbone offense stymied, three lost fumbles, and a rowdy crowd that wanted nothing more than to see the mighty Tide fall from the undefeated ranks.

Through all these hardships, it would have been easy in those last few moments for Bryant to say, "You know, there's no way we can win this game; I think we'll just quit." What if All-American guard John Hannah had decided to give half the effort because he thought they were beaten? What if defensive end Mike DuBose had only gone half-speed on his hit of Tennessee quarterback Condredge Holloway; would he have caused a fumble? If Tide defensive stalwart John Mitchell had already thrown in the towel, would he have been alert enough to recover the fumble that set up Alabama's winning touchdown?

You see, when your vision is so compelling in your life that it drives you and forces you to hang in there through the tough stuff and get over the mountains and through the valleys, then your finish will be rewarded. For Bryant and his players, this reward came in the form of a victory over rival Tennessee.

For you, hanging in there against all odds and finishing strong may result in a turnaround in your company. Or whipping a substance abuse problem. Or repairing a broken marriage. Or finally getting into medical school. You see, we must not give up on anything because giving up stays with you the rest of your life. Bryant said it this way: "The first time you quit, it's hard. The second time, it gets easier. The third time, you don't even have to think about it."

Peter Drucker, the great leadership guru, summarized leadership in one sentence: "Leadership is always about results." Coach Bryant would refer to them as wins.

After all, it was Bryant who said many times, "I ain't nothin' but a winner."

Chapter Two

COMMUNICATION SKILLS

"If you went in to talk with Coach Bryant and he said something, when you went out the door you didn't have to wonder what he meant. It was clear, and he meant it."

—WILLIE MEADOWS
Alabama Equipment Manager, 1966-86

A s important as vision is, without communication skills firmly in place, guess what is going to happen with that vision? Absolutely nothing. It will just rattle around in your brain with no place to go. It'll occupy space, drive you crazy, and give you a splitting headache. In order for your vision to become a reality, you must communicate and sell it so that "your vision" becomes "their vision."

So how do you communicate a vision? How did Coach Bryant take his visions and turn them in to his players' and coaches' visions? How did his August 1958 vision of winning the 1961 national championship also become the visions of freshmen Jimmy Sharpe, Billy Richardson, Billy Neighbors, Pat Trammell, Tommy Brooker, Bill Oliver and Mal Moore? For that matter, how did Bryant sell his national title visions to players of the 1964, 1965, 1973, 1978, and 1979 Tide squads, or his visions of winning SEC championships to 14 different Alabama teams?

BELIEVE IT'S IMPORTANT TO COMMUNICATE

Well first, you must believe within your organization that it is important to communicate. Many organizations operate like silos, where nobody talks to anybody and you end up with dead-end communications.

Wal-Mart founder Sam Walton once said, "Communicate everything you can with your partners (a.k.a. "employees" in Wal-Mart vernacular), because the more you communicate with them, the more they'll understand, and the more they understand, the more they'll care, and once they care, there's no stopping them."

There was indeed no stopping the Alabama Athletic Department under Bryant's leadership. Caring for the school, caring for the Athletic Department, and caring for the student-athletes in all sports trickled down from above. With long-time aide Sam Bailey running the day-to-day operations of the Athletic Department, Bryant's organizational skills – legendary on the field – were put into good practice off the field. Obviously, everyone knew who the boss was.

BE VERBALLY PRECISE –
CLEAR, CONCISE, AND CORRECT

There's nothing worse than being in a 90-minute leadership session and you walk out saying, "What did they say in there? What are we supposed to take from this?"

I'm quite convinced that very few of Coach Bryant's players or coaches ever left one of his meetings scratching their heads and asking "What are we supposed to take from this?" Oh, they may have had trouble *hearing* or *understanding* what he said, but rarely did they fail to comprehend what he meant. To put it mildly, Coach Bryant had their full, undivided attention.

John Underwood, long-time *Sports Illustrated* writer and co-author of Bryant's autobiography, *Bear*, vividly illustrates this point. "I was doing a story on Coach Bryant for *Sports Illustrated*, so he let me go with the team to one of the last Alabama-Georgia Tech games," Underwood said. "I stayed in the room right next to him at the team hotel. The next morning at the team meal, I sat at a table with the head of the English department. Coach would always invite people like that on road trips to keep the whole school involved.

"Coach got up to talk to the squad and the whole room went into an oral shutdown. Bear's voice got down lower than normal and that room was riveted. He barely spoke above the growl of a whisper that he activated whenever he wanted your utmost attention. The players leaned forward in their seats, eager to hear.

"Just then, a kid moved his arm and accidentally knocked over a glass of water. The spill hitting the floor sounded like Niagara Falls. Still the room was totally focused on the head coach. After the meeting, that English professor said to me, 'If I could reach my students like that, I would teach for nothing.'"

In talking with many people for this book, several common themes permeated the conversations – Bryant's physical stature, his motivational techniques, the famous practice tower, his equally famous office couch, and, unequivocally, his unmistakable, low, mumbling, raspy voice. Listen in as they remember.

"The sound of his voice set him apart. You knew he was in the room," said Buddy Aydelette, an offensive tackle in the late 1970s.

"His commanding voice made people think – Shh, Shh, he's going to say something," said Jimmy Bank, a Bryant family friend and son of long-time Alabama radio network producer and World War II hero Bert Bank.

Sylvester Croom, who played for Bryant in 1971-1974 and coached for him from1976-82, said, "Coach *sounded* like a bear. He had that deep voice that I couldn't understand at first. But I figured it out real fast. He'd speak to us in a low mumble and that worked to his advantage because we had to be dead silent and listen to him intently in order to understand what he was saying."

"Coach had a rough sounding gravelly voice and when he spoke, you listened," said All-American defensive end John Croyle.

Keith Dunnavant, author of *Coach: The Life of Paul "Bear" Bryant*, said Bryant had "the voice of God."

"Coach had a real dense voice," said Clem Gryska, an assistant for Bryant for 17 seasons from 1960-76. "You had to really listen closely to him, but he did that on purpose so the players would listen."

Charlie Land, who covered Bryant for many years as sport editor and later publisher of *The Tuscaloosa News*, said, "That low rumbling voice of his made him a forceful guy."

"Coach was a man of few words," said rival Tennessee head coach Johnny Majors, who had a 1-5 record against Bryant. "He didn't try to out-talk people, but if he had something important to say, people would listen and gravitate to him."

Bud Moore, an end on Bryant's 1958-60 squads, said, "Coach had a purpose to everything he did. At team meetings, he'd mumble to the squad on purpose. The players up front heard him, but the others were trying to figure out what he said. And the coaches were, too. He could talk loud when he needed to. I think there were two reasons he'd do that. First, it forced everyone to be quiet and listen, and second, it created a team atmosphere. All the players would check with each other to see what was going on."

All-American Billy Neighbors, who was in Bryant's first freshman class and later a member of the 1961 national championship squad, said, "He had an unreal voice. When he walked in, you were awed by it."

"He was a big man and he mumbled on purpose, I believe," said Wes Neighbors, Billy's son and a redshirt freshman on Bryant's last team in 1982. "He'd make you lean over and listen. Everything he did had a purpose."

"Coach had this long, deep, gruff voice," said Larry Ruffin, a mid-1970s offensive lineman. "As players, we listened and did what he told us. We knew we'd win if we listened and carried out his instructions."

Jeff Rutledge, quarterback for Bryant's 1978 national championship team, said, "He was intimidating with that deep rolling voice. You had to pay attention when he spoke to you."

Another national championship quarterback was Richard Todd of the high-powered 1973 unit. "Coach had a real low voice with kind of a mumble," he said. "You'd better be real quiet and listen or else you might miss something important."

Gary White, a student manager in 1959-61 and long-time Athletic Department administrator, said, "Coach spoke in a low, gruff voice, but always in a humble manner."

"He was a big man with this deep, growly voice," said All-American defensive back Tommy Wilcox, a member of Bryant's last four teams in 1979-82. "A lot of times I couldn't understand him, so I'd just smile."

At times, Bryant didn't even have to say a word to get his players' and coaches' attention; just the mere *anticipation* of his mysterious voice left them hanging. Bum Phillips, former NFL head coach at Houston and New Orleans, was an assistant coach for Bryant at Texas

A&M in 1956-57. To this day, Phillips recalls Bryant's uncanny ability to communicate.

"Coach would walk in a little late to a coaches' clinic or one of our staff meetings and everybody would quit talking," Phillips said. "He'd walk in very slow and sit down. He might just sit there for a minute or two; sometimes he might smoke a whole cigarette while we waited. No one would speak until he spoke.

"And once he started talking," Phillips continued, "he had the unique ability to capture everyone's attention and hold it. He didn't talk too much like so many leaders do. Coach knew just the right amount. He had complete confidence in what he was saying, so he wasn't afraid to stop talking and just hesitate and pause. He didn't yap a lot and that made people listen to him because they felt he had something important to say. Some leaders just talk too much. Coach Bryant never did."

Today, almost 28 years after Bryant's death, his rumbling, low voice is heard at every Crimson Tide home football game during pre-game festivities, accompanied on the video boards by famous plays during his Alabama career. When this pre-game ritual began several years ago, Alabama students listened in bewilderment, trying their best to understand him.

Only after *The Crimson White*, Alabama's student newspaper, published Bryant's entire pre-game spiel did the students learn what he was saying. On that day, a new language – "Bryant-Speak" – was discovered by a new generation of Tide fans.

OPTIMISM

Where would any leader be today without optimism? Nowhere. I'm not even sure they could be called a leader if they don't have optimism. As we learned earlier, it is critical that a leader has vision, and it's important to spread that vision and make it contagious. However, for followers to have hope for the future, the leader must exude optimism as part of the vision. Vision is headed nowhere without optimism. Who wants to be part of a vision that's destined to die with pessimism?

Coach Bryant dealt with optimism in an interesting way. Publicly, he made you think his Crimson Tide wasn't even going to show up on game day. You might as well sell your tickets and stay at home, he'd say, because you sure weren't going to get your money's worth. Injuries, lack of focus, lack of talent, players not taking the game seriously, distractions, you name it; Bryant was notorious for poor-mouthing his teams, while at the same time building up his opponents.

Mickey Herskowitz, in his book, *The Legend of Bear Bryant*, said, "He (Bryant) didn't exactly invent the art of poor mouthing, but he advanced it considerably."

Prior to the 1976 Liberty Bowl, following a 9-3 "down" year (by Alabama standards at least), Bryant one-upped UCLA head coach Terry Donahue in the poor-mouthing battle. After Donahue's glowing tribute to the Alabama program and how honored he was to be going up against the greatest coach of all time, Bryant shot back. "When I heard who we were playing," Bryant said, "I thought they meant the University of Central Louisiana. When I found out what UCLA really stood for, it almost scared me to death." Alabama routed the Bruins, 36-6.

Publically, Bryant was indeed a poor-mouther. Privately, though, to his coaches and players, Bryant was the eternal optimist. There wasn't a game on Alabama's schedule that he didn't think they could win. Never was there a "Picture Day" – as he called the opening day of fall practice – when he wasn't optimistic about his team winning the SEC title or the national championship.

Optimism can certainly be used as a tool to motivate, and soon we'll see many stories of how Bryant motivated his players. Utilizing pure optimism to motivate, though, Bryant was at his best prior to the 1966 Orange Bowl, when his fourth-ranked 8-1-1 Tide squad was to face a 10-0 and third-ranked Nebraska team. Bryant describes the scenario in his book, *Bear*.

"I put it up on the board for the players, charting how it would happen," wrote Bryant, whose "little boys" were out-weighed by "those big fine-looking Nebraska players" by 30-35 pounds per man. "UCLA would upset Michigan State (in the Rose Bowl), LSU would upset Arkansas (in the Cotton Bowl), and we would play Nebraska (that night) for all the marbles. It wouldn't happen again in a million years, but that's exactly the way it went...."

At halftime, with Alabama comfortably ahead, 24-7, an Orange Bowl committee member informed Bryant that UCLA had indeed held on to upset Michigan State. "Men," Bryant told his troops, "UCLA upset Michigan State 14-12. It's all there for you to take." Bryant's "once in a million years" optimism turned into reality as the Tide ripped the Cornhuskers, 39-28, to capture the 1965 national crown.

MOTIVATION & INSPIRATION

Motivating and inspiring people are part of any leader's job description. There's just no way this can be ignored. As much time as you put in at the office, as much planning as you do, as much vision as you may have, as optimistic as you are about your company, or your local United Way board, or your child's P.T.A., if you don't have employees or volunteers who are motivated and inspired, you might as well throw it all out the window. Without your troops being motivated and inspired, months or even years of hard work can evaporate quickly.

Leadership expert Gil Peterson, in his book, *The Master Plan for Leaders: a Biblical Perspective*, says this about motivation:

> *Motivation has been defined as "getting others to do what you want them to do, because they want to do it." Motivation has as a basic root the word "motive." That is what is inside a person that causes them to consider a concept, cause, or action. Clarity is needed to get an idea across, but for the person to accept it and make it their own, the person must see the idea as something that they can and should do. The leader must not only explain what needs to be done, but inspire the followers to give it their best. Motivation is basic to teamwork.*

This definition fits Coach Bryant perfectly. He did it all – he recruited players who were already self-motivated when they stepped on campus; he provided clarity in his teachings and actions; he inspired his players to give it their all; and he stressed the teamwork concept.

Perhaps retired Florida State head coach Bobby Bowden says it best. "Bear Bryant was the best leader I was ever around," said Bowden, who never faced Bryant on the field, but revered him for years. "He was in command of everything. He could get more out of an individual than even that person thought he had. Whatever you had, Bear would get it out of you, and more."

Motivating his football players was always on Bryant's mind. To him, Xs and Os were useless without proper motivation. Game plans meant nothing if he couldn't get his teams on board and committed to a purpose. Visions of conference and national championships would have remained only visions if not for his motivating power.

On a subject that probably deserves an entire book, we'll look at a few ways Bryant motivated his players and coaches. Although we'll only scratch the surface, it'll be worth the ride.

Before we can examine how Bryant motivated people, though, we must first analyze where Bryant's motivation came from. Without a doubt, it can be traced all the way back to Moro Bottom, Arkansas, on the family farm. Making their living from the soil of the earth and the toil of their hands, the Bryant family learned hard work, pride, dedication, discipline, and respect.

Bryant's noble upbringing was one about which novels are written, but throughout his coaching career, he made clear what kept him motivated. "Football has never been just a game to me – never," he said. "I knew it from the time it got me out of Moro Bottom, and that's one of the things that motivated me – that fear of going back to plowing and driving those mules and chopping cotton for fifty cents a day…"

Preston Gothard, one of Bryant's last signees in the early 1980s, believes this background made Bryant the motivational leader he was. "Coach Bryant's tough background gave him a special knack to relate to people of all levels – rich and poor, well-educated or not, black and white, and so on," Gothard said. "He knew people from all walks of life, and to him there was no class of people. He had a keen understanding of human nature."

From 1932-35, while an outstanding player for the Crimson Tide, Bryant's motivation came from several folks, especially head coach Frank Thomas, a product of the legendary Knute Rockne at Notre Dame. Thomas' top assistant was Hank Crisp, who had recruited Bryant from Arkansas and was Thomas' designated good cop/bad cop.

Bryant's philosophies on motivation may have been birthed, or certainly enhanced, in the fall of 1935. In Alabama's game with Mississippi State, Bryant broke his fibula and was not expected to play the next week against Tennessee. He was allowed to dress, though, and in Crisp's pre-game pep talk, he addressed the players and said, according to *Bear*, "I'll tell you gentlemen one thing. I don't know about the rest of you... but I know one thing. Old 34 will be after 'em, he'll be after their butts."

Because the coaches changed most of the players' numbers each week, Bryant didn't even know who "Old 34" was until he looked down and saw it on his jersey. With spirits soaring, Bryant went out and played one of his finest games ever as a Tide player, broken leg and all. No one could have known it at the time, but that type of motivational technique would become a Bryant trademark for the next 46 years.

Bryant's first head coaching job was shortly after World War II, when he led the Maryland Terrapins to a 6-2-1 record in 1945. To this day, his Maryland players hold Bryant in high reverence, especially his motivational skills.

"Coach was an inspiration and motivator and he fit into our lives perfectly," said fullback Harry Bonk. "He was just right for us. Some days he was so tough you hated him and thought, 'I will never come back out here.' But the next day, you loved him and were right back out there. He taught us a lot and it was much more than just football."

Joe Drach, a tackle and defensive end for the Terrapins, experienced during a game what had to be a déjà vu moment for Bryant. "Coach had a way of inspiring you," said Drach, who once described Bryant as "violently laid back." "He could get every bit of talent out of every one of his players. He had played hurt himself, so playing with pain was part of it.

"One game, I broke my hand and after Coach examined it at halftime, he grabbed it and pressed it against the wall until the bone popped back in place. I taped it up and played the whole second half.

"After the game, he said that the team had needed me and that we would have lost without me. After he said that, I would've gone out and broken another bone just to show him I could've done it again. Who else but Coach Bryant could get you to do that?"

Bryant's quarterback at Maryland was Victor Turyn, who cites as his motivation Bryant's survival-of-the-fittest mentality. "During practice, Coach would pair us off one-on-one to practice tackling and blocking," he said. "I'd get after it with our fullback, Harry Bonk, a big 200-pounder. We'd just kill each other. I had a scab on my nose all year because we didn't have face masks in those days. I can still hear Coach Bryant yell down at us and say, 'Cut out that lovey-dovey stuff and let me hear that leather crack.' Then he'd put us through a bunch of wind sprints. Just surviving was motivation enough for me."

Bryant's quick exit from Maryland landed him in Lexington, Kentucky, where he guided the Kentucky Wildcats to a 60-23-6 record and the 1950 SEC Championship. Bryant's Kentucky players share similar stories about their coach's motivation and inspiration.

"Coach didn't just have one way of leading," said All-American quarterback Babe Parilli. "If you lost a game and it seemed like the end of the world, the next week he might not work you as hard. If we won, he'd work you even harder. I guess he didn't want us to get too overconfident."

Steve Meilinger, a Wildcat end in 1951-53, said, "Coach Bryant was a great leader because he was a great psychologist and motivator. Before the start of my senior season in 1953, he called me into his office and said, 'Steve, you know what? You can't make this team. I don't know where I can play you.' Boy, that got me really pumped up and made me want to do better. I only went out and made All-SEC and All-American that year."

Howard Schnellenberger was a tight end at Kentucky in the early 1950s and later coached as an assistant at Alabama under Bryant. "Coach Bryant placed a high value on winning and not being out-hustled," said Schnellenberger, who at 76 years old is head coach at Florida Atlantic University. "He'd put enough fear in you, so you'd do what he said."

Dick Rushing, a Wildcat fullback for Bryant, said, "If there was a big wall out there and Coach asked you to knock it down, you felt you could do it because he put such faith in you. You realized he had faith in you or he wouldn't have asked you in the first place."

After eight seasons, Bryant left the bluegrass of Kentucky for the prairie of Texas A&M. One of his inherited Aggie sophomores was Gene Stallings, who would play for him at A&M, coach with him at Alabama, and eventually become Tide head coach from 1990-96.

Stallings humorously recalls a motivation story from 1954, Bryant's first season at A&M. "After our Junction training camp, we play our first game and lose to Texas Tech, 41-9," Stallings said. "The following Monday, when we go down to practice, all of our game gear was in our lockers, which was unusual because we didn't normally put on game gear on Mondays. The manager comes running around and says, 'Coach Bryant said, "Put on your game gear and go out on Kyle Field." Well, you didn't practice on Kyle Field; that's where you played.

"So we put on our game gear and like a bunch of little sheep, we all go out there. Coach Bryant's out there singing *Jesus Loves Me*. I said, 'Lord, we're in trouble now.'

"He calls us up and without us loosening up or stretching or anything, he said, 'The ball's right there. We're going to take up right where we left off Saturday night.' Now, *that* was a bad practice. We didn't get beat 41-9 anymore."

Stallings was right; Bryant's motivation of his downtrodden Aggies worked like a charm, although it didn't show in their final 1-9 record. But, after that 32-point loss to Texas Tech in the opener, the Aggies' average defeat was by less than seven points per game, including five single-digit losses. Without a doubt, Bryant's motivational techniques in 1954 laid the groundwork for his 25-4-2 record at A&M over the next three seasons.

Motivation might sometimes be a marathon, not a sprint. You might not see results overnight, and certainly other factors play a role in how effective your motivation can be. For Bryant's players at Texas A&M, they may have been motivated and inspired that first season, but without a level playing field, they had no chance until Bryant could recruit better players. (We'll save his recruiting prowess for a later chapter.)

Although Bryant laid his coaching foundation at Maryland, Kentucky, and Texas A&M, it was at Alabama where he became the superstar, the giant in his field, and the greatest college coach of all time. Listening to many of his players, coaches, and associates talk about how he motivated and inspired them was for me a real treasure.

Frank Broyles, long-time Arkansas head coach and athletic director, competed against Bryant many times and was forever captivated by him. "Paul knew how to motivate young athletes – physically, mentally and emotionally," Broyles said. "There were two phases of his approach. At Kentucky and A&M, he did it by fear, and he had a lot of dropouts along the way.

"At Alabama, he still used fear, but he also motivated by encouragement. Everything he accomplished at Alabama was based on encouragement to his players in all areas of their lives. He perfected this method and as a result got peak performances from his athletes and helped them reach their highest level of individual skill and team play. He was the greatest coach of all time at doing this."

Dave Sington, Bryant's first captain in 1958, said, "We had an innate fear of Coach. He was a real tough guy, but he made you want to play for him. He knew how to motivate players – who to prod and who to praise. We heard him say, 'There's only one way to do it – the Bryant way.' Then he'd say, 'There's only one clique on this team – the Bryant clique.'"

Leon Fuller, a defensive back for the Tide in 1959-60, said, "I only weighed 150 pounds and was not a great athlete. I played halfback, defensive back, ran back punts, and held snaps for our place kickers. I realized that if you tried hard, Coach Bryant would use you in the game. He appreciated players who would give an all-out effort. It didn't matter if you weren't a great athlete. I saw a lot of talented athletes who he didn't use because they didn't give the effort he demanded."

Halfback Billy Richardson said, "Coach would motivate by fear a lot, but he'd get the best out of guys. We all knew he'd been a rough, tough player at Alabama and he played with a lot of courage."

Jimmy Sharpe spent 16 years under Bryant's tutelage, four years as a player and 12 as an assistant coach. In one of the many "halftime locker room" stories I heard, Sharpe said, "The ground-level foundation for Alabama's winning tradition under Coach Bryant was set during the 1960 Alabama-Tennessee game in Knoxville. We were behind, 14-0, at the half and Coach Bryant came through the locker room door ranting and raving and slamming doors and kicking things. We were scared to death and didn't know what he might do. Well, he got our attention. Although we ended up losing the game, 20-7, we really outplayed Tennessee in the second half.

"A few weeks later we went to Atlanta to play Georgia Tech, and we were behind, 15-0, at halftime," Sharpe continued. "It was the same situation as before. The locker room was totally silent. The coaches were backed up against the wall. No one was moving around. We waited for Coach Bryant, and we thought we knew what to expect.

"All of a sudden he came in and said, 'Hot dog, we've got them right where we want them!' He patted us on the backs and handed out Cokes and towels and told us we were going to win the game, and we believed him. We won it, 16-15, with a field goal on the last play of the game.

"Those two games, as far as I'm concerned, set the foundation for Coach Bryant at Alabama. They proved to us that we could win. We believed in Coach Bryant and ourselves from that point on."

Bill Battle, a 1960-62 letterman and later head coach at Tennessee, said, "Coach Bryant knew how to sell the plans he'd created. He was the boss and fear was a big part of his motivation. He had an uncanny ability to take players when they were down and lift them up. Then he could turn around and bring the cocky ones down to earth."

Lee Roy Jordan, perhaps the greatest of Bryant's linebackers, marvels at Bryant and how he was able to get the most out of his players. "Coach Bryant mastered the perfect combination for success at the collegiate level, or maybe developed it," said Jordan, an All-Pro linebacker for the Dallas Cowboys and a member of the College Football Hall of Fame. "He inspired us to be the best we could be as players, students and individuals. He did that by pushing us to the limit — to a level we didn't know existed.

"Fear of failing him was important in the formula, but after pushing you until you dropped, he'd come over to you, put an arm around your shoulders and say, 'I just want you to be the best you can be. I know what's inside you. I know what you're capable of doing on the football field.'

"When you got a compliment like that from Coach Bryant, or just a pat on the back, you wanted to melt on the spot. Moments like that would overwhelm you and make you more determined to play that much harder for him."

The oldest of the Davis family of kickers is Tim, a 1961-63 letterman. Tim's father, Arkansas native Alvin "Pig" Davis, played for Alabama in the late 1930s when Bryant was an Alabama assistant coach under Frank Thomas. For years, the families remained close. "If you gave Coach a hundred percent, he'd give you 100 percent back for life," Tim said. "He wanted to take care of his boys. His players would die for him."

Eddie Versprille, a fullback for the Tide in the early 1960s, said, "When Coach said something, you did it and you didn't ask why. The man knew how to push your buttons. During my junior year, we were practicing and Coach was up in his tower. The next thing I knew he was yelling at me. He'd seen something he didn't like and told me to take off my starter's jersey. I was demoted right on the spot.

"Then he barked, 'You helped us win last year, but if you don't shape up, you can go right back to Norfolk.' I got the message and shaped up real quickly."

To this day, All-American quarterback Joe Namath marvels at Bryant's ability to connect with his players. "Coach had the ability to communicate to us what he thought was right," Namath said. "I came from Pennsylvania. We had guys from Florida, Tennessee, and of course, Alabama, and he knew how to connect with all of us. He knew us and how to push the right buttons with each player."

Larry "Dink" Wall, a fullback in 1961-64, recalls an example of Bryant's vision (as discussed in Chapter One) *and* motivation, all rolled into one. "Coach was able to get you to believe that you were a lot better than you really were," Wall said. "He would plant subtle seeds in your mind.

"In 1961, our first championship season, he told us, 'If we go undefeated, you'll win this thing.' Well, after each game we won, we began to realize that if he told you something, it generally would come true. To be a leader you've got to be able to motivate people and he could do that."

Mickey Andrews, a 1963-64 Tide letterman and for years Bobby Bowden's defensive coordinator at Florida State, recalls Bryant's "pushing-your-limits" philosophy. "Coach Bryant had a unique way of making you better than you thought if you'd sacrifice and do things the right way," Andrews said. "He wanted to know what your limit was and not many people can do that by themselves. He was great at creating an environment that allowed you to feel safe letting him push you to your limits."

All-American Paul Crane, Bryant's center in 1963-65, said, "Coach Bryant had a knack for knowing how to motivate individual players. One guy might need a kick in the butt while another would need a pat on the back. He knew what type of motivation each one of us needed, but he required the same effort from all of us. Coach was tough and hard, but we all felt he was fair. When you got a compliment from him, you deserved it."

Leon Ashford, a student athletic trainer from 1966-70, said, "Coach created a sense that you didn't want to disappoint him. If you messed up in practice, you hoped he was watching someone else. He created a sense of urgency in you to perform in such a way that would please him. That's a remarkable quality in a leader."

One of Alabama's all-time favorite players is All-American Johnny Musso, a running back in 1969-71. Musso explains Bryant's unique ability to motivate. "I've seen quotes about Vince Lombardi treating everyone the same – like dogs – but Coach Bryant didn't treat everyone the same," Musso said. "He treated everyone fairly, but not the same. Yes, he motivated the team as a whole, but motivating each of his players individually was where he excelled. He had an uncanny insight into what each and every player needed.

"For me, it was encouragement the whole way. He gave me the opportunity to do exactly what I needed to do in order to be successful. I'm not quite sure how he knew that, but he did. His encouragement to me personally was so powerful that I never wanted to displease him. And because of wanting to please him all the time, I'd like to think I was at my best at all times."

In the mid-1960s, Bryant created an everlasting tradition in *The Bear Bryant Show*, where he and co-host Charley Thornton would captivate an entire state for a solid hour. Fans tuned in to see the previous day's highlights; players tuned in to hopefully hear a mention of their names.

"On Sundays we'd get in a workout and then rush over to see *The Bear Bryant Show* on TV," said Pat Raines, a three-year center from 1970-72. "One Saturday, we beat Florida and I had played my best game. I couldn't wait for Coach to roll the film and tell the world I was the best the SEC had to offer. Instead, I heard him say, 'Pat Raines played about as well as he could.' That's how he used praise to keep pushing and motivating you."

On Wednesday evenings during the season, Bryant would gather his team together for what amounted to be a fireside chat. John Mitchell, the first black player to play in a varsity game for Bryant and Alabama in 1971, remembers one particular meeting and Bryant's motivational genius.

"I remember one year during Tennessee week, we gathered on Wednesday night for a squad meeting with Coach," said Mitchell, who at the time was an assistant coach for the Tide. "He didn't talk long, but went into his spiel on what it meant to wear that crimson shirt when he was a player and how much it meant to play Tennessee. He said, 'I hated to lose to them. If we didn't win, I couldn't kiss my mama or hug my dad. I just couldn't do it because I had let them down. So, if you love your parents you'll go out and beat Tennessee this Saturday.' We killed them, 30-7. Coach definitely knew how to motivate his players."

In describing Bryant's motivational skills, Tide receiver Dexter Wood said, "Coach Bryant was a master psychologist. He had 85 different personalities on his squad every year and he knew exactly how to push everyone's buttons to maximize their potential. Some guys got his encouragement and with others he'd beat them down at times, but it was an unbelievable knack he had."

As we've learned, Bryant wasn't a man of many words. So, when a few good ones came someone's way, they noticed. "Coach knew what motivated you," said Alan Pizzitola, a defensive back in 1973-75. "And he would do what it took to hit the right buttons. With one guy, he might come down off that tower and grab his facemask and shake him. If I intercepted a pass, he might holler on that bullhorn, 'Nice hands, Pizzitola!' I was good for two weeks after that."

A common Bryant technique was to demote a player, whether deserving or not, to see how he would react. We've already heard Eddie Versprille's story, and we'll see several more in upcoming pages.

Another such victim was Ricky Davis, an early 1970s defensive back. "After my junior year, I was riding high and then we got to spring practice," Davis said. "I got to practice one day and saw that I was placed on the second team defense. I was upset and confused. I went with the second group and went full blast when we were only supposed to go at half speed. No one said a word to me. I went to dinner than night still upset.

"The next day at practice I was listed back on the first team. Later on, I asked (defensive backfield) Coach (Bill) Oliver why they did that to me. He said, 'Coach Bryant likes to do that once every four or five years. He wanted to see how you would react. Would you pout or work harder? You handled it the right way.'"

Larry Ruffin, an offensive guard in 1973-75, recalls Bryant's motivation one time in the form of *concern*. "Before my senior year I was in great shape," Ruffin said. "I was up to 235 and at the peak of condition, ready for a great season. I got real sick that summer and ended up in the hospital. I lost 40 pounds and was really in tough shape.

"One day, Coach called my hospital room to check on me. His last words were: 'Four weeks to practice. I'm counting on you.' I got so fired up. I got some weights and started lifting in the hospital bed with IVs stuck in me. I got my family to bring in a steak to eat. It took five painful hours to finish it, but I got it done. Coach could get you to do those kinds of things. I reported to camp at 195 and kept grinding it out the whole year."

Les Fowler, a defensive back in the mid-1970s, says Bryant's reputation alone was enough to keep the players motivated. "When we got to Alabama in the mid-70s, Coach Bryant led more by reputation," said Fowler, currently one of Alabama's team orthopedic surgeons. "We were all Alabama kids who had heard about Bear Bryant all our lives. We all wanted to please him and wanted him to be proud of us. We didn't want to let him down. He was a proven winner by then and if we lost, it was our fault."

Thus far, we've heard several references to Bryant "pushing" his players, or getting the most possible out of them. Rickey Gilliland, a linebacker from 1976-78, marvels at this particular Bryant trait. "Coach had the innate ability to look in your eyes and know exactly how far to push us to see if we'd quit or not," Gilliland said. "He was experienced and seasoned and knew his profession of football – and the people playing for him – inside out."

Timing was everything with Bryant. He knew just when to peak his players and when not to. "Coach Bryant motivated you to prepare and give your best every practice, even though those practices weren't much fun," said Dewey Mitchell, a mid-1970s linebacker. "His best talks were on Monday, Tuesday, and Wednesday. They were designed to motivate you to practice hard that day.

"Saturday was not the day to get motivated. It would be too late then. Coach was so good at getting you to reach your peak while you were preparing. The games came naturally after that."

K.J. Lazenby, who served eight years under Bryant as a player, a graduate assistant and an assistant coach, adds, "Coach treated all his players fairly but not the same because what motivated me might not motivate you. I grew to learn that he knew what buttons to push. By the time I was with Coach, he'd mellowed some, but his intensity toward the game was still there. He knew how to love one and kick another. And regardless of when you played for him, he hated to lose."

One of the most celebrated players in Alabama football history is Ozzie Newsome. Playing from 1974-77 in a run-oriented wishbone formation, Newsome caught 102 passes in his entire Alabama career, yet still made first-team All-American in 1977. Even for an All-American, someone you'd think needed no motivation, Bryant was not sparing. It was just another example of Bryant's brilliance.

"In the fall of my senior year," Newsome said, "I came back as the big man on campus. I was a pre-season All-American and expected to be a high draft pick. On the first day of practice, we had to do a conditioning run. I did my four quarters in less than 90 seconds, so I passed without a problem. I made my time easy.

"We did several photo shoots right after that and I was posing with Coach. We were only together for five minutes, but he said to me, 'You need to be out front; I saw a little senior strut in that workout you had. You've got to be leading us all year. I don't want you resting on your laurels.' It didn't matter who you were; Coach wouldn't tolerate complacency."

Murray Legg, one of the many heroes on the famous "Goal Line Stand" series against Penn State in the 1979 Sugar Bowl, said, "Coach never had many discipline problems and that was because of the fear factor with him. Nobody wanted his wrath or his punishment.

"His leadership filtered down to the team, which helped us produce leaders. In 1976, we had high expectations, but after four games we were only 2-2. After Georgia beat us, 21-0, he was fed up and really went off on us: 'You're a disgrace to anyone who wore the Alabama uniform; you're a disgrace to your mothers and fathers.' On and on he went. That was on a Saturday night. His final words were, 'I thought we had some leaders on this team. I leave it up to you. You will be dressed in pads and on the field at 8 a.m. tomorrow. Breakfast is mandatory.' With that he walked out.

"That was a huge turning point of the season. The next morning he dismissed all the assistants and said to us, 'You all are mine.' He put the ball on the 40 and said, 'I want the first team offense and the first team defense out here.' We then went through the most intense three-hour scrimmage of all time. It was either kill or be killed. It worked. We ended up 9-3 and beat UCLA in the Liberty Bowl."

Not only was this early October practice a turning point to the season, it just may have solidified two more national championships for Bryant down the road. Similar to the way Jimmy Sharpe talked about the 1960 Tennessee and Georgia Tech games helping Bryant lay the foundation for the future (including two national championships in 1964 and 1965), his turnaround in 1976 after the Georgia loss was equally important. From that point to the end of the 1979 season, Alabama won 41 of its next 44 games, three SEC championships, and two national championships.

Remember what I said earlier about motivation sometimes being a marathon and not a sprint? Bryant challenging and motivating his players – whether it was 1960 or 1976 — are examples of his brilliance, his vision, and focus. In both cases, it took years to see the results.

As mentioned earlier with Ricky Davis, Bryant would sometimes check a player's fortitude with a quiet and discreet demotion. For Bryant and his coaches, it was simply done with a pencil and eraser on a depth chart. For the unsuspecting player, though, it could be devastating.

Barry Krauss, who became an instant Alabama legend with his stop of Penn State running back Mike Guman in the 1979 Sugar Bowl, simply calls these demotions "gut checks." And Krauss should know about gut checks.

"Coach Bryant was big on the color of the practice jerseys – red for the first team, green for the second team, orange for the third team," said Krauss. "To keep you motivated, he'd put you through at least one major gut check during your playing career. He'd make you dig deep inside yourself.

"One season, I had the red jersey all week in practice and was all pumped up, but didn't start for three straight games. We went over to play at Georgia, a huge game for me. I didn't start and I'm convinced Coach wanted to find out what I was made of. Would I quit?

"Well, the next week I missed curfew and Coach caught me. I was scared to face him and when I did, I cried my eyes out, big time.

I took tears to another level. Coach kept me on the team because he was convinced I had learned that it was not about me. It was, 'What could I give to the team?' He gave me a second chance, because he saw something in me. He felt I was a big game player and that's what I was.

"We never wanted to disappoint Coach Bryant," Krauss continued. "He'd push us beyond our limits in practice and say that there'd be a time in the fourth quarter when we'd need every ounce of mental and physical toughness we could muster. 'Dig deep and take a stand,' he'd say.

"In that famous goal line stand against Penn State, when we came off the field, we just looked at him and thought, 'We did it, Coach.' He didn't have to say a word because he knew we had done our jobs."

Offensive lineman Buddy Aydelette, whose Alabama teams finished 34-2 during his three letter years, cites Bryant's psychological talents in motivating his players. "Coach was a motivator," Aydelette said. "He'd tell us that we were playing for more than ourselves. He'd say, 'You're playing for your school, your parents, and your hometown.' He'd come up with some story about the other team wanting it more than we did. Whatever it took, he'd do it."

Byron Braggs, a defensive lineman in 1977-80, recalls another of Bryant's pep talks during Tennessee week. "Coach Bryant was a master motivator," Braggs said. "My senior season (1980), on Wednesday night of Tennessee week, he called a meeting and told us a story about three kinds of people: 1) the Winner, 2) the Loser, and 3) the Also-Ran. He was really getting to us and firing up our emotions.

"At the end of the message, Coach just collapsed in his chair and I thought he was having a heart attack. I looked around and half the room was in tears and the other half looked like they wanted to kill something right then. And we still had to practice on Thursday. We went out in sweats and still got people hurt. We were back in our room that night sitting on our beds and my roommate looked like a caged animal ready to run through a wall.

"We went up to Tennessee and killed them (27-0). They didn't get a first down until halfway through the third quarter. The Tennessee fans gave us an ovation."

Defensive back Jim Bob Harris had the honor of playing on two national championship teams in 1978-79 and in Coach Bryant's famous "315" game in 1981, when Bryant became the winningest college football coach of all time. As with many other players, Harris cites fear as Bryant's primary motivation tactic.

"Coach got through to us partly out of fear and partly out of intimidation," Harris said. "But our biggest fear was disappointing him. I wanted him to be proud of me and pat me on the head with a big grin on his face and say, 'Atta boy.' It's mind-boggling to think of the influence he had on all of us."

One of Harris' partners in the defensive backfield for three years was All-American Tommy Wilcox, who said, "Coach Bryant would always get the most out of you, and he'd do it in subtle ways. Some, he'd have to kick in the tail. With others, he'd do it with words. And some didn't need much at all. The man was a great psychologist who could work with all types. The main thing was he could get you to do more than you thought you could do."

Joey Jones, a speedy receiver for Bryant in 1980-82 and for Ray Perkins in 1983, said, "Coach Bryant made you believe you could do things you never dreamed you could achieve. I weighed 170 pounds and I'd go into games thinking that no one could cover me and that I could knock down anyone 100 pounds heavier than me. When Coach believed in you, your confidence shot up immediately."

Kurt Schmissrauter, a lineman in 1981-83, recalls Bryant's challenging his players to be their very best. "Coach Bryant would pick you out and see where you would break long before you played in a game," Schmissrauter said. "He'd put you through the wringer out there in the heat of the practice field or he'd demote you, and it was all designed to see how you would react to adversity.

"We learned that every day was not a bed of roses and you had to figure out how to get back up when you got knocked down. Nothing in life would be more physically demanding or mentally challenging than playing football for Coach Bryant at the University of Alabama."

In the 1982 Alabama-Tennessee game in Knoxville, punt returner Darryl White received a shot of Bryant's motivation, but not after a scare. "I caught a punt on the 12-yard line and was mowed down by a bunch of Tennessee players," White said. "The ball popped out and somehow, someway, I was able to recover it on about the one-yard line.

"As I was coming off the field, I had to run right by Coach Bryant. He just tapped me with his rolled-up paper and said, 'That's all right; don't worry about it.' Because he didn't get all fired up at me, it gave me a sense of confidence and motivated me to go back out there and not be worried about making another mistake."

Of my more than 200 interviews with people who knew Bryant, this one small nugget from Alan Gray set off a few light bulbs in my brain, giving me the first of many "Aha!" moments during my study of this great coach.

"Coach would test you and it was always directed at an *individual*, not all eleven guys," said Gray, a quarterback in 1978-81. "He would motivate us all by singling out one particular person. As a freshman, I didn't pick up on this, but as a junior and senior, I saw it. I'd think, 'Ah, it's *his* day today.'

"But Coach was looking to see how that guy would respond. Great leaders know how to motivate and he was one of the best. He knew that if you were tested and proven during the week, you'd play at your very best on Saturday. Coach would tell us, 'If I get you ready to play on Friday, that's my fault. My job is to get you ready to play on Saturday.'"

Rich Wingo's "day" (as Alan Gray calls it) of reckoning came during opening week of the 1977 season. On a day he says changed his life forever, Wingo found out the hard way how it was to be singled out, tested, and proven by Bryant, all in a matter of hours.

"The best thing Coach Bryant did for me was kick me off the team," said Wingo, a native of Elkhart, Indiana, only 20 miles from Notre Dame's campus. "Right before my junior season, someone made the terrible mistake of voting me to be a pre-season All-American, and I began to think that I *was* a pre-season All-American.

"It was a normal practice and we were in linebacker drills, where Coach Bill Oliver would throw one of us the ball and we'd sprint off the field. I'm sure I wasn't hustling, although I certainly wasn't consciously thinking about it. After doing that several times, Coach Bryant said, 'Wingo, get out there and do it again.' That's the first time he had ever made me do a drill again. Everybody got completely quiet. So I got out there by myself, in a linebacker stance.

"Coach Oliver said, 'Hut,' he threw me the ball, I sprinted to the sideline, then gave Coach Oliver the ball back. Coach Bryant said, 'Do it again.' You could have heard a pin drop. I did it again, and Coach said, 'Get off my field.' So I started jogging off the field. After about 20 steps, I looked back and everybody was just staring at me. That's when I realized I had been kicked off the team.

"I went to the showers and my friend Tim Garl, one of the student trainers, came in and said, 'Do you realize you've just been kicked off the team? No one's ever been kicked off the team and allowed back on except Joe Namath. And you ain't no Joe Namath.'

"I got dressed and waited for Coach Bryant after practice," Wingo continued. "He asked me what I was doing there. I told him that my dad told me before I left home years ago that no one's going to fight for Rich Wingo any longer except for Rich Wingo. I said, 'I'm here to fight.'

"He let me come into his office and he told me to sit down. I had been on that couch too many times – for the wrong reasons – so I sat in a chair right next to his desk. We spoke – well, *he* spoke – for an hour and five minutes. I'll never forget it as long as I live. All the time he's talking, I'm thinking, *'Am I on the team or off the team? How am I going to tell my parents?'*

"So he's leaning back in his chair, smoking that Chesterfield, and he says, 'Rich, I think you're a good football player. And I think I'm a good coach. They say you're a pre-season All-American, but that doesn't mean squat to me. I just don't know if I want you on my football team.' He was blunt.

"He explained to me that I was just *content* with being the starting inside linebacker and that's the way I'd play. He said he wanted people on his team and those around him to be *committed* instead of *content*, people who wanted to get a little better every single day. For the first time, I realized exactly what he was talking about.

"So he put his hand on the phone and said, 'Tell me where you want to go. You want to go home, back to Notre Dame? One phone call and you can be there tomorrow. Michigan? Ohio State? Back to the schools that recruited you? One phone call. As a matter of fact, if you want to stay in school here, we'll pay your way through school. I just don't know if I want you on my football team.'

"I just sat there, not saying a word," Wingo continued. "Finally, I said, 'Coach, this is my family. This is my fourth year. If I can't play here, I don't want to play anywhere.' He looked at me and said, 'I'm going to go home and pray about it and talk to (wife) Mary Harmon about it.'

"Then he said, 'Be in my office tomorrow at nine o'clock and I'll tell you what I'm going to do. It'll be my decision.' I got up and left.

"That conversation impacted my life. The concept of being *committed* and not *content* is a major part of my testimony today. He wanted people who were totally sold out on the program. He said, 'Rich, I'll take people who aren't the best athletes, but I'll win with those guys if they're sold out every day.' He was telling me that he didn't think he could win with me. It just crushed me.

"So I met him at his parking spot the next morning at six a.m. He got out of the car and slammed me right off the bat. He said, 'I thought I told you nine o'clock.' I just came right back at him and said, 'I'll wait.' I figured I didn't have anything to lose.

"He said, 'Follow me to my office.' So I followed him up that steep coliseum stairwell. It took forever; he wasn't the fastest walker. We got to his office, he closed the door behind us, and said, 'Mister, if you want to be on this football team, you be on that field today and we'll pretend like nothing ever happened. And if you don't, that's fine with me. It's your choice. Now, get out of my office and close the door.'

"I went out to practice that day thinking I'd be way down on the depth chart and would have to work my way back up. Well, I was still the starting inside linebacker, just as he said, like nothing had ever happened. Starting that day, I went from being *content* to being *committed.* I learned how to practice and get better every day. He took a chance on me, because he certainly had ten guys who could take my place.

"All my friends told me that after they saw me jog off the field that day, they had the best practice of their entire career at Alabama, because they didn't know who was next."

Bryant's willingness to take chances in testing a player's commitment was a constant gamble. If Krauss or Wingo, or the many others whom he tested, had buckled during those face-to-face meetings with him, they would have no longer been a part of the University of Alabama football program. And who knows, without Krauss (#77) and Wingo (#36), would there have ever been a Goal Line Stand against Penn State? Knowing Bryant and his motivation techniques, probably so. Other players would have risen to the occasion and stood in the gap.

Wingo's story of contentment versus commitment doesn't end there. For several years, curiosity got the best of him, so he just had to eventually pop the question.

"After I graduated and was playing in the NFL, Coach Bryant would always want to see me when I was back in Tuscaloosa," said Wingo, who played seven seasons as middle linebacker for the Green Bay Packers. "Finally one time, I worked up enough guts to ask him, 'Coach, why did you kick me off the team?'

"You see, a year or so after I left, one of the assistant coaches told me that Coach had *planned* to kick me off the team that day, to gut-check me, to see how I would react. So I said, 'Coach, I want to know if you had it planned, or if I really wasn't hustling out there that day.'

"With a big smile on his face, he said, 'Oh, Rich, you're smart enough to figure that out, aren't you?' To this day, I still don't know the answer."

What a great lesson we can learn from Rich's story. Are you just *content* with what you do, or are you *committed* to what you do? This applies in every facet of your life – job, career, home, family, church, charities, relationships, faith, and so on. What will it take to get you from being content to being committed?

As I mentioned earlier, an entire book could be written solely on Bryant's motivational skills. I think motivational *power* may be a better word. As we come toward the end of this chapter, I want to leave you with a few more stories, including one from the son of an Alabama football icon, several from media members who covered Bryant, and one from a player who was a part of Bryant's historic last game.

Jim Goostree, long-time athletic trainer for Bryant, was without a doubt Bryant's go-to guy on and off the field. Officially, Goostree was the trainer. Unofficially, he was the disciplinarian, the strength coach, the bed checker, the meal planner, and the team's travel agent. When hair length was an issue for the players in the late 1960s and early 1970s, he was even dubbed the "hair coach." Stories abound about Goostree and his toughness, especially with the injured players. Many had rather play hurt than to face Goostree in the training room.

Goostree's son, Jimmy Tom, grew up around the inner sanctum of Alabama football and has many fond memories of Bryant. "My dad was with Coach Bryant for more than 25 years and Coach depended on him," said Goostree, who as an artist has drawn many portraits of Bryant.

"Coach Bryant had the gift of discernment. He knew the different personalities of his players and knew which ones to kick in the pants or put an arm around. He was a master motivator and at first he did it by fear, but as the years went on you could see him lighten up and he learned to motivate so his players became self-motivated."

Throughout Bryant's career, media members marveled at his abilities as a coach, a psychologist, a disciplinarian, a servant, and of course, a motivator. Listen in as several reminisce about his motivation.

"Coach Bryant treated all the players the same, yet in different ways," said Allen Barra, author of the classic Bryant biography, *The Last Coach*. "He knew the particular needs of each player and what it took to motivate him."

Another Bryant biographer is Keith Dunnavant, author of *Coach: The Life of Paul "Bear" Bryant* and *The Missing Ring*, a story about the undefeated and uncrowned 1966 Tide squad. "Coach Bryant really understood human nature and was a magnet for a certain type kid," Dunnavant said. "He loved to work with overachievers, players who didn't have enormous talent, but had enormous desire.

"He was a master with that type of guy because he knew how to identify with him. That was central to his success. He could look into that kid and figure out what motivated him. Then he could push his buttons to the edge without pushing him over."

Cecil Hurt, sports editor of *The Tuscaloosa News*, covered Bryant for three years in the early 1980s and Bryant's legacy for the past 27 years. "Coach Bryant was a very good judge on how to motivate his players," Hurt said. "He had learned over the years that some could take harsh criticism and others needed to be dealt with more gently. He had developed the ability to judge motivational needs and then use either the iron hand or the velvet glove."

Delbert Reed, author of *Paul "Bear" Bryant: What Made Him a Winner*, which provides an in-depth study of Bryant and his rare combination of personality and skill, said, "Coach had a gift for motivating people, and mainly that came by simply asking them to do whatever it was that needed doing.

"Those many qualities make up a leader, and because of all these qualities and many more, Coach Bryant was able to teach, inspire, and help others to reach greater levels of achievement than they might otherwise have reached."

Charlie Land, former sports editor and publisher of *The Tuscaloosa News*, believes Alabama's tradition of proclaiming "fourth quarter's ours" originated from Bryant's motivating his players to finish strong. "Coach got a lot done psychologically on the practice field," Land said. "He'd push his players past what they thought they could do. It was punishing in a way. Then in a tough game in the fourth quarter, those players believed they could do anything he asked of them."

Birmingham News sportswriter Clyde Bolton covered Bryant and Alabama for more than 20 years and offers an interesting perspective on Bryant. "Coach was an enigma to me," said Bolton, who in 1972 authored the first definitive history of Alabama football, *The Crimson Tide*. "People say he was a great coach because he was a great motivator. Well, there were a lot of coaches who could motivate.

"Others would say it was because he worked hard, but a lot of coaches worked hard. Or that he was a great Xs and Os man, but there were a lot of them, too.

"Bobby Marks, one of his former players and assistants, once said, 'I don't know what Coach Bryant had, but he had a lot of it.' I can't help but agree."

On December 15, 1982, at the end of his 39-year head coaching career, Bryant announced his retirement as Alabama head football coach. Two weeks later, an entire nation tuned in as he coached his final game in the Liberty Bowl, a 21-15 victory over Illinois.

Johnny Brooker, a backup kicker, recalls the special moment and Bryant's last motivational tug at his team's heart strings. "At the Liberty Bowl, Coach was getting all kinds of press coverage," Brooker said. "Reporters were everywhere. They looked like ants crawling over an ant hill that had just been busted up.

"At our last big meeting with Coach Bryant before the game, he was apologizing to us because he was receiving all the publicity and attention, and not us. He started to cry because he said it wasn't fair to us.

"If seeing him shed a tear didn't bring a lump in your throat, then you didn't have any feelings. After that, I don't think we could have lost the ball game if we had wanted to. He asked us not to go out and win the ball game for him, but to play for ourselves and our mamas and papas and the school. We were representing them and he wanted us to make sure we did well for them.

"He wanted us to play the best we were capable of playing. That's all he asked of us. Well, we just couldn't lose. We couldn't let the win-ningest coach in college football end his career on a sour note. We were motivated to win for him beyond belief. We wanted him to go out a winner and he did, too."

PUBLIC SPEAKER

Leaders must understand that leadership generally gravitates to the man or woman who can talk. That's generally who we elect to our political offices. That's who we hire as our CEOs; it's who we want as our head coaches.

The ability to stand up in front of a group, command attention, and really work hard in becoming an effective public speaker is to whom we relate.

The best public speakers do it by telling stories. They are yarn spinners; they're anecdote collectors; they understand that people are hard-wired to retain stories, not PowerPoint presentations.

I think it would be safe to say that Coach Bryant never won any elocutionary awards from the National Speakers Association. But at the end of the day, he was an incredibly effective public speaker. He commanded and owned a room. When he spoke, everything stopped.

As we'll see in Chapter Three, Bryant made himself available and visible to many large groups on many different occasions. So for this segment, we'll recount just one story that Bryant told at a Touchdown Club meeting many years before his death. Although some believe this story is an Internet embellishment, it was confirmed as fact by long-time Chattanooga sportswriter Roy Exum, who covered Bryant for many years.

This story exemplifies exactly what kind of person Bryant was, both on and off the field. In it, we learn from him the invaluable leadership trait that "It don't cost nuthin' to be nice."

I had just been named the new head coach at Alabama and was off in my old car down in South Alabama recruiting a prospect who was supposed to have been a pretty good player and I was havin' trouble finding the place.

Getting hungry I spied an old cinder block building with a small sign out front that simply said "Restaurant." I pull up, go in and every head in the place turns to stare at me. Seems I'm the only white fella in the place. But the food smelled good so I skip a table and go up to a cement bar and sit. A big ol' man in a tee shirt and cap comes over and says, "What do you need?"

I told him I needed lunch and what did they have today? He says, "You probably won't like it here, today we're having chitlins, collard greens and black eyed peas with cornbread. I'll bet you don't even know what chitlins (small intestines of hogs prepared as food in the deep South) are, do you?"

I looked him square in the eye and said, "I'm from Arkansas. I've probably eaten a mile of them. Sounds like I'm in the right place."

They all smiled as he left to serve me up a big plate. When he comes back he says, "You ain't from around here then?" I explain I'm the new football coach up in Tuscaloosa at the University and I'm here to find whatever that boy's name was and he says, "Yeah I've heard of him, he's supposed to be pretty good."

And he gives me directions to the school so I can meet him and his coach. As I'm paying up to leave, I remember my manners and leave a tip, not too big to be flashy, but a good one and he told me lunch was on him, but I told him for a lunch that good, I felt I should pay.

The big man asked me if I had a photograph or something he could hang up to show I'd been there. I was so new that I didn't have any yet. It really wasn't that big a thing back then to be asked for, but I took a napkin and wrote his name and address on it and told him I'd get him one.

I met the kid I was lookin' for later that afternoon and I don't remember his name, but do remember I didn't think much of him when I met him. I had wasted a day, or so I thought.

When I got back to Tuscaloosa late that night, I took that napkin from my shirt pocket and put it under my keys so I wouldn't forget it. Back then I was excited that anybody would want a picture of me. The next day, we found a picture and I wrote on it, "Thanks for the best lunch I've ever had."

Now let's go a whole buncha years down the road. Now we have black players at Alabama and I'm back down in that part of the country scouting an offensive lineman we sure needed. Y'all remember (and I forget the name, but it's not important to the story), well anyway, he's got two friends going to Auburn and he tells me he's got his heart set on Auburn too, so I leave empty handed and go on and see some others while I'm down there.

Two days later, I'm in my office in Tuscaloosa and the phone rings and it's this kid who just turned me down, and he says, "Coach, do you still want me at Alabama?"

And I said, "Yes, I sure do."

And he says OK, he'll come.

And I say, "Well, son, what changed your mind?"

And he said, "When my grandpa found out that I had a chance to play for you and said no, he pitched a fit and told me I wasn't going nowhere but Alabama, and wasn't playing for nobody but you. He thinks a lot of you and has ever since y'all met."

Well, I didn't know his granddad from Adam's housecat so I asked him who his granddaddy was and he said, "You probably don't remember him, but you ate in his restaurant your first year at Alabama and you sent him a picture that he's had hung in that place ever since.

"That picture's his pride and joy and he still tells everybody about the day that Bear Bryant came in and had chitlins with him. My grandpa said that when you left there, he never expected you to remember him or to send him that picture, but you kept your word to him and to Grandpa that's everything. He said you could teach me more than football and I had to play for a man like you, so I guess I'm going to."

I was floored. But I learned that the lessons my Mama taught me were always right. It don't cost nuthin' to be nice. It don't cost nuthin' to do the right thing most of the time, and it costs a lot to lose your good name by breakin' your word to someone.

When I went back to sign that boy, I looked up his Grandpa and he's still running that place, but it looks a lot better now and he didn't have chitlins that day, but he had some ribs that woulda made Dreamland proud and I made sure I posed for a lot of pictures. And don't think I didn't leave some new ones for him, too, along with a signed football.

I made it clear to all my assistants to keep this story and these lessons in mind when they're out on the road. If you remember anything else from me, remember this:

It really doesn't cost anything to be nice, and the rewards can be unimaginable.

Chapter Three

PEOPLE SKILLS

"As a leader, Bear Bryant always took up for his people. If you were part of his team, he had your back and would never desert you."
—LARRY GUEST, *The Orlando Sentinel*

Great leaders have a heart for people; they care about other people; they're interested in people; they have empathy for people; they love people. Without a doubt, Coach Bryant earned check marks for all of the above.

Eddie Robinson, the great Grambling coach, said you have to coach every player as if he were going to marry your daughter. He said, "You can't coach 'em if you don't love 'em."

Great coaches and great leaders definitely have an interest and desire to work with people. Coaches can't coach from their offices or homes. They can't give their team a pep talk on a conference call or webcam. Coaches must be out there among their players – on the field, at the dining hall, and in team meetings.

Coaches must also be out there among the alumni, boosters, and fans. Whether it's a spring golf tour, or an alumni chapter meeting, or the local Kiwanis Club, or the state's largest Quarterback Club, if they want their program to get maximum exposure, they must be out among the people.

So, what did Coach Bryant teach us about people skills? Let's find out.

VISIBLE & AVAILABLE

There's a tendency with top level leaders to get up in an ivory tower and shoot e-mails across their empire. Rarely does this leader come down among the common folks. How effective as a leader can he be if there's no personal relationship with his workers, or in the case of a coach, his players and fans?

From George Washington to Abraham Lincoln to Martin Luther King, Jr. to Mother Teresa, these leaders were all out among the people. Business management guru and author Tom Peters calls it "managing by walking around."

But long before Tom Peters came along, Coach Bryant understood that. I'm quite sure there's never been a coach in the history of college football that was more visible and available than Bryant.

John Croyle, an All-American defensive end for the Tide in the early 1970s, tells a powerful, yet humorous story about Bryant's availability and visibility. First, let me say that John is one special person. When we talked for this book, he brought me to tears after telling me what he's done since his playing days at Alabama.

In 1974, John founded the Big Oak Boys Ranch near his hometown of Gadsden, Alabama, and in the early 1990s he opened the Big Oak Girls Ranch near Springville, Alabama. Since 1974, more than 1,700 abused, neglected, and forgotten children have called the Big Oak Ranches their home. If you're looking for a leader in our society today, not to mention a bona fide American hero, then John's your man.

One of the first people with whom Croyle shared his ranch vision was Coach Bryant. "I had this idea and dream about a ranch for neglected children here in Alabama," Croyle said. "I went to Coach Bryant to get his views on it. In the middle of the meeting his secretary, Rebecca, came in and said, 'I've got Bob Hope, Roone Arledge, and Spiro Agnew all on hold. What should I do?'

"Coach said, 'Tell them to wait.' Then he turned back to me and said, 'Now tell me more about your ranch idea.' He made me feel like the most important person in the world. He always told us that his players took precedence over anybody else. That day he proved to me that he backed up what he said. His message to me was, 'Go build the ranch. Follow your dreams.' He knew I was built to do this."

The "Rebecca" to whom John referred is Rebecca Christian, Bryant's long-time secretary, who confirmed Bryant's open-door availability for his players. "He was like a father to all of his players and kept up with them long after they'd graduated and became adults," she said. "Whenever they needed to see him, they'd just knock on his door and go right in. They never had to go through me.

"As Coach got older, though, those two-a-days would wear on him. He had 5 a.m. practices and I don't see how he did it. It was so hot in the summer and he kept up such a stiff pace. He'd leave me a note that he was taking a nap and when to wake him up. So he'd shut the door and get some sleep. If the door stayed open, people would just wander in to meet him so they could brag later that they'd met Coach Bryant."

Clem Gryska, an assistant coach for Bryant from 1960-76, recalls a similar time when Bryant put notoriety and royalty on hold for his team. "In 1981, Coach Bryant broke Amos Alonzo Stagg's record with a win over Auburn in Birmingham," Gryska said. "In the locker room afterward, we had a little team prayer and then Coach started his talk with the team.

"Just then, a school official came over to tell him that President Ronald Reagan was on the phone. Coach said, 'Tell him to wait until I've finished talking with my team.' Availability to his team always came first, even before the President of the United States."

Bryant's availability to his players didn't start at Alabama. Lou Karibo, who played for Bryant at Kentucky in 1952-53 and coached with him at Texas A&M, said, "When we first got to Texas A&M, Coach told the players one day, 'If you have any personal problems, just come see me.'

"Well, the next day there was a line a mile long waiting to see him. It looked like the confessional line on the day before Easter. I pulled all the players together the next day and told them, 'Let me explain what a personal problem is. It's if your mother or father dies.'"

Marlin "Scooter" Dyess, a tiny but quick running back for Alabama in 1957-59, recalls Bryant using these office visits to inspire his players. "I was 148 pounds at the time, but with great speed," said Dyess, whom Bryant dubbed the hero of Alabama's 10-0 win over Auburn in 1959. "Coach got word to us that he wanted to meet with all of us one-on-one and to come to his office when we had a free hour in the day. I walked down the hallway, hoping I'd see him there so I wouldn't have to go into his office. Sure enough, I saw him walking right toward me.

"I stammered out, 'Coach, I'm Scooter Dyess. I understand you want to meet with me.' He put his hand on top of my crewcut and said, 'Who are you, the water boy?'

"He ushered me into his office and told me he'd seen some films of me in action. 'You played well,' he said. I answered, 'I thought I should've played more, but the coaches were afraid I'd get hurt.' Then he said, 'I don't care who gets hurt. I'll play the guy who can get the ball across the goal line and I don't care what size he is.'"

Defensive back Mike Clements, one of the unsung heroes of the famous "Goal Line Stand" in the 1979 Sugar Bowl, has a humorous perspective of Bryant's availability. "Coach Bryant would tell us, 'Come to me with your problems. My door will be wide open.' I always wished I had a problem big enough to justify going in there. I always wanted to walk right in there and talk to him, but I never could come up with a problem to justify going in."

Bryant enjoyed being with his players. He wanted to know how their classes were going, how their folks back home were, and updates on their girlfriends. Due to his position and power, though, the feeling may not have been mutual.

"At the dining hall in Bryant Hall, the assistant coaches would all sit together," said David McMakin, a defensive back in the early 1970s. "Coach Bryant wouldn't do that. He'd stand in line just like the rest of us. He'd get his food and then start peering around the room and end up sitting at a different table, each meal with a different group of guys. Of course, we were always praying it wouldn't be our table because that was definitely going to alter our conversations."

Not only was Bryant accessible to his players, but he was highly visible to the Alabama fans as well. In the off-season, he'd juggle appearances at civic clubs, touchdown clubs, booster meetings, and golf events. After all, he was the face and voice of the Alabama football program, and the more people who heard his message, the better it was for the University of Alabama.

Bryant loved golf and in the late 1950s joined Tuscaloosa's fledgling Indian Hills Country Club. If Bryant had a personal golf coach he could call his own, especially in his early years at Alabama, Jackie Maness was his man. Once the Tide golf team started practicing at Indian Hills in the early 1960s, Maness and Bryant became friends. When Alabama was in need of a head golf coach, Bryant chose Maness, who served from 1964-68. Maness recalls Bryant's visibility and availability at an event in Pensacola, not to mention his round of a lifetime.

"One day," Maness said, "Coach called me up and said, 'Jackie, they want me to play in the celebrity pro-am at the Pensacola Open. I can't go play golf in front of all those people. I'll make a fool of myself.' I said, 'Coach, you should go do that. It's all for a good charity. Let me make a call and see what's going on.' I checked on it and discovered they had paired him up with Doug Sanders. I called Coach back and told him, 'It's all set. You're with Doug Sanders and he'll look out for you.'

"Coach went down to play and I went along also and rode around with him. He had a par on the first hole with hundreds of people watching and you could see him begin to relax. He loosened up and played a great round of golf that day. He shot a 79, as I recall."

Of all the Crimson Tide booster groups to whom Bryant spoke through the years, none is any more famous than the one in Bridgeport, Pennsylvania, a town located about 20 minutes from Philadelphia. Founded in 1970 by Tony "Chick" Chiccino, who had played for Bryant at Kentucky and was a teammate of Alabama assistant coach Larry "Dude" Hennessey, the Bridgeport Boosters have been led for years by Chiccino's brother-in-law, Johnny Nicola.

The bubbly Nicola, whose club puts a congratulatory billboard on a busy Philadelphia thoroughfare any time Alabama wins a national championship, recalls Bryant's availability on a cold and snowy Philadelphia night in December of 1979. "I had been inviting Coach up to our booster club in Philadelphia," said Nicola, who stills takes a group every year to an Alabama home game. "He finally said he would come. On the day of the banquet, we had an 18-inch blizzard. Everybody kept wondering if he was coming. I called his office and he insisted on making the trip, despite the terrible weather.

"Well, Coach made it. We had 600 people that night and he stayed and signed autographs for all of them. At one point I said, 'Coach, do you want to stop?' He said, 'No, Johnny. These people came out in a snow storm to see me, so it's the least I can do.'"

Whether they were aware, or whether it was a stroke of Bryant's genius, or both, Bryant was a master at using the media to enhance his visibility to the masses. Listen in as a few reminisce.

"Bear Bryant had something rare as a leader – personality and chemistry," said former *Birmingham Post Herald* sports editor Bill Lumpkin. "Everyone liked him – the press, coaches, the media, alumni, and so forth. Everyone wanted to please him, which was a huge motivational factor that he possessed."

Birmingham News sportswriter Clyde Bolton recalls Bryant's feelings toward the media softening as his career progressed. "I first started covering Coach Bryant in 1961," Bolton said. "In those days he'd give you short answers and start looking at his watch to hurry you along. He was kind of tyrannical with the media and viewed us as a necessary evil or sometimes an unnecessary evil. In his later years, he began to mellow and be more concerned with his legacy. He developed a kindly grandfather approach. He'd laugh with us more and dealt with us at a more human level."

Paul Finebaum, a print and radio broadcasting icon in Alabama and around the southeast, said, "I was a 24-year old cub reporter in Birmingham the day Coach Bryant retired. I thought, 'It doesn't get any bigger or better than this.' Coach knew who I was because he was very attuned to get his message out to the public in the proper fashion. He was very careful in that regard."

John Pruett, former sports editor of *The Huntsville Times*, said, "Coach Bryant was an excellent interview over the telephone which wasn't true of all coaches. He was also good at returning calls to the media which doesn't always happen."

The extremely comical Beano Cook, long-time college football analyst for ESPN, puts Bryant's visibility into perspective. "The man put more coaches on the unemployment line, but no one disliked him," he said. "It's amazing!"

So, whether you're the president of your company, or the garden club, or your fraternity at college, you need to be visible and available to those who work or volunteer for you. They'll appreciate you more, and in the process, you will be humbled by the experience.

LISTEN & ASK QUESTIONS

The highest compliment you can pay anybody is to listen to them and truly focus on them in an uninterrupted fashion. To me, it's the ultimate people skill.

Equally important is to ask them questions, like, "What do *you* think? How are things going with *you*? What would *you* do if *you* were in my situation? How would *you* make this call?"

Great leaders are not threatened by listening and asking questions. As we'll see, neither was Coach Bryant.

Paul Dietzel, an assistant coach under Bryant at Kentucky in 1951-52 and later head coach at LSU, Army, and South Carolina, remembers Bryant as a true listener, especially in staff meetings. "I had coached for Sid Gilman at the University of Cincinnati," said Dietzel, to whom Bryant gave the nickname "Pablo" because, as Bryant said, "We can't have two Pauls on this staff."

"Sid was a true football genius and I think Coach Bryant hired me at Kentucky because I knew Sid's offense and he wanted to install it. When I was coaching with Gilman, we had very open staff discussions. Everyone expressed their opinions and we'd argue things out.

"With Coach Bryant, you'd have the floor but there'd be no arguments. One day we were discussing how to block an end. When it was my turn, Coach said, 'What do you think, Pablo?' I had my ideas, which were different than his and when I finished, he said, 'OK, we'll try it.' After the meeting, another assistant said, 'That's the first time anyone has ever disagreed with Coach.' I think things loosened up after that."

Jim Dent, author of the book *Junction Boys*, said, "Bear is viewed as this totalitarian leader who ruled with an iron fist. However, one thing is overlooked and I learned this in interviewing those Junction players. He included a lot of people in his decisions. He was always asking his players and coaches for their opinions even when they didn't know he was doing it. Coach Bryant would canvass people before making key decisions. He was a good listener."

Bobby Smith, one of Bryant's first quarterbacks at Alabama, lets us know that Bryant had a knack for listening to his players. "In our first players' meeting, he walked in and, wow, what a presence he had," said Smith, who along with Dave Sington served as Bryant's first team captain. "He started talking and it wasn't about football. He started asking us questions – 'How many of you wrote your mama this week? How many said your prayers?' We were all just stunned."

Bud Moore and Bill "Brother" Oliver were teammates on Bryant's 1958-60 Tide teams and later served as Alabama assistant coaches. Both recall Bryant's willingness to listen. "He was a good listener," Moore said. "I played under him and then coached for him and he cared about what you had to say."

Oliver, echoing Moore's thoughts, said, "Coach was the best listener I've ever seen in my life. He'd give all his assistants the chance to give him our opinion."

Alabama linebacker Jackie Sherrill, who later became head coach at Pittsburgh, Texas A&M, and Mississippi State, said, "As a leader, Coach listened instead of speaking. He listened and observed and didn't talk much. He could tell more about you than you ever knew."

Sylvester Croom, a player and assistant coach for Bryant, has sat in hundreds of staff meetings in his long coaching career, but none stand out more than Bryant's. "Coach cared about his players," said Croom, who was Mississippi State's head coach from 2004-08 and is now an assistant with the NFL's St. Louis Rams. "He had a servant's mentality and wanted to contribute to the lives of the young men he coached. He wanted to do what benefited the individual and the group. Whenever we were trying to make a decision about a player, he'd get all of our opinions. Then he'd say, 'When you decide, do what's best for the player, because that's what's best for the program.'"

Mike McKenzie, who covered Bryant for 12 seasons at *The Huntsville Times*, *The Tuscaloosa News*, and *The Baton Rouge Morning Advocate*, said, "Coach was old-school. He played fundamental, grind-it-out football, but surrounded himself with great assistant coaches who were extremely loyal to him. He listened to them and was willing to adjust to changes that were going on in football and society. Some coaches couldn't do that."

Without question, Keith Jackson will forever be *the* television voice of college football. Through his many years calling Alabama games for ABC-Television, Jackson and Bryant became friends. From a media standpoint, Jackson said, "Coach Bryant was a very good listener. When you asked him a question, he'd take his time before he answered. He would study the subject carefully before saying a word."

If you want to make your workers or volunteers feel important, just ask their opinion about something and then listen intently to what they say. You may not agree with them, and their idea may never see the light of day, but that's fine. The opportunity you've given them to express their opinion will give them such a lift that you'll both benefit from it in the end.

EMPOWER

Great leaders empower people; they uplift people; they give them inner strength; they exhort them; they lead cheers for people; they're not afraid to give them compliments.

Empower. Just the word sends chills down my spine. There's a reason the word "power" is part of "empower." It gives people a rush like they've never seen or felt before. It makes them more assertive and more confident.

We've learned how Coach Bryant motivated his players, but for the most part, motivation is for a particular moment in time or a particular issue at hand. Empowerment can last a lifetime, and no college football coach was better at empowering his troops than Bryant.

"Coach Bryant never missed an opportunity to praise a coach or player," said Pat Dye, an Alabama assistant under Bryant from 1965-73 and later head coach at East Carolina, Wyoming, and Auburn. "In a team meeting, he'd point out something you came up with to help win the game, even if it was his idea to begin with. I never heard him criticize a quarterback in a team meeting. He would get on his best players who were strong enough to take it and then the others would fall in line."

Howard Schnellenberger, who played for Bryant at Kentucky and coached with him at Alabama from 1961-65, said, "Coach knew how to correct a player and give him hard punishment. If that kid responded the right way and didn't pout, Coach would put an arm around him and tell him how improved he was and great he could be."

Benny Nelson, a halfback from 1961-63, shares a memory of Bryant from the 1963 Orange Bowl and how he empowered the entire squad. "The night before the game, both teams were at a big banquet," Nelson said. "Bud Wilkinson, the Oklahoma coach, had a program and recognized his players by their name, number and hometown.

"Then Coach Bryant got up and without looking at a note, rattled off every player, his number, and hometown. It meant a lot to us. Everyone commented later that they couldn't believe how he did that."

Gaylon McCollough, Tide center in 1961-64 and author of the book *The Long Shadow of Coach Paul "Bear" Bryant*, said, "Everyone wanted to please Coach — his players, coaches, ticket takers, secretaries. We all wanted his recognition and a pat on the back."

All-American receiver Dennis Homan, who caught passes from Tide quarterbacks Steve Sloan and Kenny Stabler, said, "We wanted to receive his praise and to hear him say, 'Good job.' That spoke volumes to us."

John Croyle, whose job at his Big Oak Ranches is to empower kids every day, said, "Coach Bryant was not a gusher when it came to praise. He didn't run around praising everybody and everything. When our unit came off the field and we'd done well, he'd say, 'Good job.' That's all we needed to hear.

"As a leader, it's important to know how to praise and when to praise. If you are always praising, it doesn't mean much. Make your praise mean something. I like sugar, but not a whole truckload of it."

So far, we've mentioned several players who had to visit Bryant in his office; some for good reasons, and some for bad. Ronny Robertson, a member of the 1973 national championship team, recalls a visit to Bryant's office he was dreading to make, but one that has stayed with him for a lifetime.

"I came to Alabama as a linebacker and a pre-dental student," said Robertson, now Associate Athletic Director for Development at Alabama. "However, as a freshman I didn't make my grades and wasn't eligible. That meant summer school and I still didn't make my grades.

"The assistant coaches told me I had to break the news to Coach Bryant. I asked, 'How do I do that?' They said, 'He's here by 5:30 a.m. Go see him then.' So I got up early one day. I saw one light on in the building, and it was his. I was scared to death as I knocked on his door.

"He ushered me in and asked what was going on. Before I could say a word, he asked, 'How are your mama and papa doing?' Then he offered me a seat on that infamous couch, but I told him I'd stand.

"I told him I hadn't made my grades and at that point I broke down and started sobbing. In fact, I was crying so hard I was heaving and choking on my tears. The next thing I knew, Coach had his arms around me hugging me like a baby. He said, 'Aw now, we'll count this as your redshirt year. You'll have to leave Bryant Hall and live with the ordinary folks. *But get those arms built up.*'"

I asked Robertson if he and Barry Krauss had compared their Bryant office crying stories, and they have. "I remind Barry that I got a hug and he didn't," Robertson said.

Ray Maxwell, an offensive lineman in 1973-75, cherished words of praise from Bryant. "As a leader, he had all that knowledge and experience," Maxwell said. "We didn't want to do anything to make him look bad. You always knew where you stood with him and never wanted to cross that line. A compliment from him made you feel ten feet tall."

Bob Baumhower, a member of the "Redwood Forest" defensive line in the mid-1970s, was another who had to make a dreaded visit to Bryant's office. "I had some size and ability and just got by on that," Baumhower said. "I had some success in the spring after my freshman season and thought I had it made. I did nothing that summer and in the fall, it showed.

"I went down on the depth chart and decided to quit. Coach got word to me and summoned me to his office. Coach said, 'What are you doing here?' I told him why and he said, 'I don't talk to quitters, but well, since you're here, sit down.'

"That meeting changed my life. At that point I had no vision for my life or career. I just went day-to-day and had no long-term vision. Then Coach said, 'So you're not happy where you are on the depth chart. Well, what did you do to get better this summer?' Then he pointed out all the guys ahead of me who had done something to get better.

"Then he said, 'Bob, I don't think you're a quitter. I just think you don't know what it takes to be the best.' Up to that point, I hadn't had much direction and motivation in my life. But that session with Coach changed the entire direction of my life and career."

Steadman Shealy, starting quarterback for Alabama's 1979 national championship squad, a graduate assistant coach in 1980-81, and co-host of *The Bear Bryant Show* in 1982, was empowered by one particular trait of Bryant. "Coach always said to 'Always expect the unexpected,'" Shealy said. "As a lawyer I live with that concept every day. I have his picture in my office and it reminds me to demand excellence of myself all the time. I will always be one of Coach Bryant's boys and I never want to disappoint him or let him down. I want him to always be proud of me."

Similar words are spoken by All-American defensive back Tommy Wilcox. "None of us wanted to let him down," Wilcox said. "We wanted to hear him say, 'Good job.' He was just like your parents that way. We always wanted to hear words of praise from him."

Three opposing coaches of Bryant's recognized his ability to empower his players and those around him. "Coach energized everyone in the Alabama program including students, faculty, fans, media, and so forth," said Frank Broyles, former Arkansas coach and for many years Keith Jackson's television broadcasting partner. "He knew how to win people over to gain support for the program. As a recruiter he won over high school coaches and parents of the players and he did it by encouragement. No one has ever equaled him as an encourager."

One of the few coaches who had a winning record against Bryant was Ara Parseghian, head coach at Notre Dame from 1964-74. "Coach Bryant understood people," said Parseghian, whose teams defeated Alabama in back-to-back bowl games following the 1973 and 1974 regular seasons. "He knew how to encourage players, coaches, and alumni, and then unite all of them for one common cause. That was his strongest asset."

Johnny Majors of rival Tennessee said, "Every person I've ever met who played for Coach Bryant was in awe of him and had great respect for him. They'd do anything to please him and do anything to not displease him. And they were always excited when they got a word of praise from him."

Jimmy Smothers, long-time sports editor of *The Gadsden Times*, covered Bryant for his entire Alabama career and was a friend of the Bryant family. He relates a lesson on praise to which we can all relate.

"Coach Bryant was a tough disciplinarian and stories got around about how he would come down off his coaching tower when he was displeased with something," Smothers said. "People also enjoyed hearing him brag on players during his Sunday television broadcast.

"In explaining a situation I'd had one time with a writer at work, I asked him about regaining a man's respect after jumping all over him. He told me to never criticize a man personally in front of others, but if something needed to be said, to do it privately. 'Then, the first time he does something worthy of praise, do it publicly,' he said. 'But,' he warned, 'Never give false praise. The individual will know if you are sincere or not.' After that, I always followed that advice in dealing with others."

DELEGATE

People-oriented leaders are never afraid to delegate.

But, here's the problem. Many leaders think they can do a job better than anybody else, so they hesitate to delegate. They don't want to be perceived as absent on the job or not earning their paycheck. Or, they just might not have total trust in letting anyone else do it.

Delegating is a real struggle with top level leaders. But, based on what I've heard from so many of Bryant's players, coaches, and associates, I'm convinced, without a doubt, that he was a terrific delegator. As great a head coach as he was, even Bryant couldn't have won six national championships by himself.

"I want coaches who are brighter than I am," Bryant often said. "If they're not brighter than I am, I don't need them."

Jimmy Tom Goostree, son of long-time Alabama athletic trainer Jim Goostree, said, "Coach was very effective in delegating authority to his assistants and then leaving them alone. He didn't tag along behind them micro-managing their activities. He'd check up on things periodically, but that was it. As a result, he made them better leaders. Great leaders can do that.

"Delegating was what made him so successful. He'd hire good people and then let them do their jobs. On any given assignment he gave to you, you'd get to work on it and keep him informed on what you were doing."

Gary White was head student manager in 1959-61 and joined the administrative staff full-time in 1964. In all, White served the Alabama Athletic Department for 33 years. "Coach said he always wanted to hire people who were smarter than he was," White said. "He was very energetic and in total charge of the program, but he never second-guessed you. He was never hanging over your shoulder telling you what to do. We felt secure because he was as strong as he was and would never let anyone interfere with our jobs."

Alan Pizzitola, an early 1970s defensive back, said, "Coach wasn't afraid to hire people who were smarter than he was. He wanted people around him who knew more football than he did. In that regard, he was like the chairman of the board. He knew how to manage people."

Pat Dye shares similar feelings for Bryant's delegating abilities. "Coach was a great delegator," Dye said. "Never once did he tell me how to coach the linebackers. It was up to me to get the most out of them. He didn't second-guess or harass you. He let you be yourself and let you use your own initiative and personality. He expected results and he got them."

Kirk McNair, sports information director in the 1970s and founder of *'Bama Magazine* in 1979, said, "Coach Bryant was a good delegator. He was coaching his coaches so they could coach the players."

Jack Rutledge played for Bryant in 1958-61 and coached with him from 1966-82. "Delegating was what made Coach so successful," said Rutledge, who picked up the nickname "Governor" because of his uncanny resemblance to former Alabama governor John Patterson. "He'd hire good people and then let them do their jobs. On any given assignment he gave to you, you'd get to work on it and keep him informed on what you were doing."

Creed Gilmer, a defensive end in 1964-65, adds, "Coach Bryant coached the coaches and they coached the players. We had super assistants and they worked as hard as we did."

All-American Ozzie Newsome, who has years of experience in drafting an NFL team and hiring coaches and staff, said, "Coach would hire great assistant coaches who had top-level ability and intelligence. A lot of coaches won't do that because they get intimidated by those kinds of assistants. He'd empower you as a coach and wouldn't micromanage you. He allowed people to do their jobs."

Tide basketball All-American Wendell Hudson, Alabama's first black scholarshipped athlete in any sport, said, "We think of Coach Bryant as a great football coach, which he was, but we tend to forget he was also a top-notch athletic director. He hired good people and trusted them to run their departments well. Coach was very good at delegating authority and allowing people to do their jobs. He built up all the sports at Alabama."

CARING

Without a doubt, Coach Bryant cared for his players, just as a father would care for his own sons. Remember what Coach Eddie Robinson said earlier in this chapter: "You can't coach 'em if you don't love 'em." Well, you can't coach 'em if you don't care for 'em, either.

"Coach cared about the people who played for him and never forgot them," said Leon Fuller, a defensive back in 1959-60. "He had a genuine concern for all of us. He took the time to know each one of us and ended up knowing more about us than anyone else."

Mickey Andrews, a running back in 1962-64, adds, "Coach was demanding but he cared about you and wanted to help you."

Bryant's care for his players extended far beyond the playing field. "If a player stayed the full four or five years, Coach Bryant would do anything to help them," said quarterback Steve Sloan, a member of two national championship teams in 1964 and 1965. "He'd call about jobs and urge people to hire his players, which they usually did. A call from Coach Bryant did wonders in the job market. It was all part of his follow-up as a leader. He cared so much about his players, he'd do whatever he could to help them."

Wayne Owen, a linebacker in 1966-68, tells a poignant story of Bryant's caring heart. "My mother died five years ago," Owen said. "As loving moms do, she had accumulated some memorabilia from my time in sports. I had put it in the attic, but recently got it down to look through it. I found a carefully preserved personal note from Coach Bryant to my parents. In it he congratulated them on an academic recognition I had received. He expressed pleasure of having me on the team and expressed his appreciation for the job they had done as parents.

"This is an example of Coach Bryant's genuine concern and keen attention to detail. I've always been amazed how much he cared for us and how much of himself he invested as a coach, teacher, and mentor. He did it for the whole organization, but kept it individualized as well."

Ozzie Newsome, one of Bryant's greatest players ever, said, "Coach's greatest leadership strength was his people skills. He understood people and what made them tick. We all knew Coach Bryant cared about us."

All-American end E.J. Junior, who had the good fortune of playing on two national championship teams in 1978 and 1979, said, "Coach Bryant was very patient with his players because he cared about us. He looked at us as if we were his own sons."

Bryant's football "family" extended to more than just his players. Everyone who worked for Bryant fell under his caring umbrella, including the hard-working student managers and trainers.

James Sanderson, a student trainer in 1975-78, recalls Bryant's care and concern. "Coach Bryant genuinely cared for us," said Sanderson, now a dentist in Birmingham. "I really found this out after I graduated. While in dental school, from time to time I would have the chance to visit with him. Every time we talked, he would always bring up something from our previous conversation.

"One time I visited him in the locker room before a game. He asked me how dental school was going and I told him I was worried about a test I had coming up on Monday. In usual fashion, he looked at me and asked, 'Then, what are you doing here?' I told him I was taking a break and that I planned to leave in the fourth quarter to get back to studying.

"A few weeks later, I was walking down the hall in front of his office and he came out of his door. He asked me how I did on the test. It meant so much to me to know that he cared. It was important to him."

Defensive back Jeremiah Castille and placekicker Peter Kim echo similar thoughts. "Coach's greatest strength as a leader was his commitment to people and his love for people," Castille said. "I met him when I was 18 years old and thinking about going to Alabama. Four years later, when I walked away from Coach, I knew I had a father away from home. He just cared about people."

"He was fair to all of us," Kim said. "Regardless of the consequences, he did the right thing because he cared for us as people."

C.M. Newton, Alabama's basketball coach from 1968-80, was hired by Bryant to turn around the Alabama basketball program, which he did with flying colors. Newton's interview for this book was a greatly detailed description of Bryant as a leader, so much so that we considered using it as the book's outline.

Newton's wisdom and his admiration of Bryant will be expounded upon in later chapters, but regarding Bryant's care for others, he said, "Coach would fuss at you and could beat up on you, but deep down you knew that he genuinely cared about you. He'd show it to you in a multitude of different ways."

TALENT EVALUATOR AND DEVELOPER

Having observed Coach Bryant and Alabama from a distance, I always assumed that he had his pick each and every year of the finest high school players available. You know, the biggest and best and fastest and quickest and strongest. Basically, I figured that whomever he wanted, he got.

But in studying Coach Bryant and his ability to evaluate talent, I came away with this conclusion. Yes, he probably did get whomever he wanted. But what I found interesting is that the best football players may not have been whom Bryant *wanted*.

I could go on and on trying to explain this, but instead I'll let him do it: "Many of our teams had only three, four, or five great players," Bryant said. "I had some with only one or two. But we usually had a dozen or so guys in the fourth quarter who got to thinking they were great."

And Bryant, in his humility, summed up his entire philosophy with this quote: "I've never won a game. I've been blessed with good players who were winners."

Bryant took pride in the fact that he could take the guys with more heart than height, more spunk than speed, more willpower than weight, and more savvy than size and win football games. "I think there are a lot of coaches that do a better job with great players than I do," Bryant said. "You take those little rascals and talk to 'em good and pat 'em on the back, they'll win for you.

"I think if we win, the determining factors are those 'in-betweens,' the guys that might fall in the category that if they *think* they're good enough to win, they'll go out and win."

Wes Neighbors, a redshirt freshman on Bryant's last team in 1982, confirms Bryant's philosophy. "Great players were not Coach Bryant's specialty," said Neighbors, who won the SEC's Jacobs Award in 1986 as a senior under Ray Perkins. "He liked to coach 'in-betweens' who were great but didn't know it. Those were the guys he made great."

"Coach had an uncanny ability to pick winners," said Pat Dye. "His recruits were far from the most talented, but if a kid had some ability, Coach would make sure he lived up to his ability. Team chemistry is always good that way. Players gravitated to him."

Peter Kim, who has the distinction of scoring the last point of Bryant's coaching career, said, "Coach Bryant extracted the best out of each player to make it work for the team's success. He didn't always play the best talent, but used the players who made the whole unit perform better."

Joe Robbins, a center in 1978-80, tells a humorous story about Bryant and his recruiting. "Coach Bryant knew people," Robbins said. "His assistants hated for him to go on a recruiting visit. They'd been working for months on a kid. Coach would go to the house, spend three minutes, get up and leave and that was it. He'd say, 'We're not recruiting him.' He had spotted something he didn't like and he was usually right."

Herschel Nissenson was the Associated Press' lead college football writer for years and covered Bryant in great detail. "As a leader," Nissenson said, "Bear knew two things – get good players and win a lot of games. That will gain a lot of respect for any coach."

Steve Sprayberry, a mainstay on the offensive line for the 1973 national championship team, said, "Coach made us want to be special.

He would tell us that most people are ordinary and only a handful have special qualities. And that group was not always the most talented.

"We were all tested by Coach Bryant and were not necessarily picked because we had the most talent. He was good at making us believe in him and that if we'd sacrifice, we'd be special in life. He'd get on guys the hardest that had the most talent but wouldn't use it."

Darwin Holt, Jerry Duncan, and Barry Smith are just a few examples of the many "in-betweens" who flourished under Bryant and his system. Alabama rosters through the years are dotted with these types of players.

"My brother Jack was a great high school running back in Gainesville, Texas, and Coach Bryant came to recruit him for Texas A&M," said Holt, who lettered for the Tide in 1960-61 after transferring from Texas A&M. "Coach looked at a black and white film and saw something in me he liked. What did he see? I was a 5'-9 ½", 147-pound center. How could he look at a grainy black and white film and see a heart that would respond to his type of leadership? He just had an innate ability to look inside players and see what they were made of."

Duncan, the poster child for Bryant's little guys, said, "Coach loved the little guy. He enjoyed it when a 185-pound guy would be playing against a 235-pounder. He loved those players who were not highly recruited but wanted to play for him. I came from Sparta, North Carolina, a town of about 350 people. I had one offer and that was Alabama and that's because my high school coach sold me to Coach at a clinic. He never even saw me on film."

Smith didn't know what to expect when he arrived on campus as a freshman in fall of 1975. "I came as an 18-year old kid, scared and wondering, 'Do I belong?' But I heard that if you worked hard, never gave up or quit, Coach Bryant would find a place for you.

"My first two seasons, I kept wondering, 'Do I have a place here?' But Coach saw something in me – I could snap a football. At 185 pounds, I became a snapper. Coach believed it, so I believed it. Not many coaches would believe in me at that size, but he not only believed, he expected it from me. In three years, we never had a punt, field goal, or extra point blocked."

In reading these stories and quotes, we've learned that Bryant's methods of evaluating talent were really more about evaluating a player's heart, soul, and mind. In my more than 200 interviews for this book, Bryant's Xs and Os were rarely mentioned. Game plans, probably in archives today at the Bryant Museum, hardly made the cut. Not one person talked about how Bryant made them stronger and faster and bigger, which of course he did, but none thought it important enough to mention.

To a man, they talked about Bryant's mastery of the mental side of football, how he willed them to win, how he took the average players and made them great, how he made them better people, and how he sought "one heartbeat, one team."

That, my friends, is a great attitude to emulate and take into your workplace.

SENSE OF HUMOR & HAVING FUN

People don't want to be around a leader whose face would break if they ever smiled. If they can't joke around and have some fun, they can't lead as well. Having a sense of humor and having fun eases the tension, both for the leader and the followers.

Coach Bryant had a sharp sense of humor displayed in many ways and to many different people. "My senior year I was sitting in my dorm when I got a call from Coach's secretary," said Leon Fuller, a Tide letterman in 1959-60 and later a defensive coordinator for Darrell

Royal at Texas. "She told me I'd been named an Academic All-American. She said, 'Coach Bryant wants you to come over for a photo shoot with the Tuscaloosa paper. And wear something nice.'

"I went over as instructed. The cameras were all set up and Coach arrived to join me. His first words were, 'Well, Leon, I guess you know what this means.' I said, 'No, I don't.' He said, 'It means it's a bad year for academics.' At that point, he started laughing real loud, so I joined him. Later, I thought, 'So true, so true.'"

Several days prior to the 1979 Auburn game at Legion Field, Bryant made an off-the-cuff comment that he'd have to go back to plowing if his top-ranked Tide team lost to Auburn. During Bryant's pre-game stroll on game day, the early-arriving Auburn students started yelling, "Plow, Bear, plow."

"Coach, do you hear what they're saying?" asked long-time sports publicist Charley Thornton.

Bryant couldn't resist a small bit of humorous retaliation. "Put your arms up high, behind your back," he instructed Thornton.

With a sly grin, Bryant grabbed Thornton's arms and "plowed" him for 10 yards or so. Even the Auburn students laughed at the sight.

Clyde Bolton shares another humorous Bryant story from Legion Field. "In 1980, when Coach Bryant's 300th win was on the horizon," Bolton said, "Alabama played Kentucky in Birmingham. My writing assignment was to follow him all day. Before the games, he would walk around the playing field and study it.

"So on this day, I felt honored when he said to me, 'Come on and walk on the field with me.' Some of the Alabama students had arrived early, so when we got over to their section they all got up to applaud. Bear turned to me and said, 'Clyde, you have a lot of fans.'"

Quarterback Ken Coley recalls Bryant's sense of humor during a visit to Druid City Hospital. "I got hurt as a freshman and ended up in the hospital," Coley said. "Coach Bryant bought me a bucket of fried chicken because he told me the food wouldn't be any good there. During his visit, when he saw all these people who'd signed my cast and wrote they loved me, he grabbed a pen and wrote: *I love you, too! Paul W. Bryant.*

"They cut that out for me when the cast came off, but someone later stole it. I wish I had it today."

Ernie Accorsi, sports information director at Penn State in the late 1960s and long-time NFL executive, recalls a humorous conversation between Bryant and Penn State coach Joe Paterno the night before their 1981 matchup in State College, Pennsylvania. "I saw Bryant and Paterno together at the Friday night reception," Accorsi said. "In those days the only way to State College was on a two-lane highway. It was an arduous trip.

"At the reception, Bryant said to Joe, 'Joe, can't you do something about that road?' Joe said, 'Paul, what do you mean? This is Pennsylvania.' Bryant said, 'Can't the road be widened or replaced?' Paterno said, 'We can't do that.'

"Then Bryant said, 'Well, Joe, if I wanted a road replaced in Alabama, the governor would do it if he still wanted to be the governor.'"

Long-time ESPN college football commentator Beano Cook recalls a similar story regarding Bryant and his influence. "In 1969, ABC-TV wanted to televise the Alabama-Mississippi game at night, which turned out to be Archie Manning's breakout game," Cook said. "Roone Arledge went to Bear's office and told him, 'My engineers tell me that the candle power at Legion Field isn't strong enough. Can you get it handled for us?' Bear replied, 'If the mayor can't get it done, he won't be re-elected.'"

BE FULLY HUMAN & VULNERABLE

If you're a great leader, you need to be yourself, be human, and be transparent. Doing this builds trust and shows you are not an automaton.

"Bear would put himself down in public sometimes," said Edwin Pope, long-time sports columnist in Atlanta and Miami. "It may have been an act at times, but it came across well. He didn't have to tell you he was the boss; you already knew it."

Coach Bryant was a master at admitting his downfalls, whether he actually had them or not. He was also transparent about his feelings and was not ashamed to shed tears when so moved.

In his 1974 autobiography, *Bear*, Bryant recalls crying several times – as a teenager the day Notre Dame head coach Knute Rockne died, when Texas A&M was put on probation in the mid-1950s, when he told his Aggie players he was leaving to go to Alabama, when he was falsely accused by *The Saturday Evening Post* of fixing the 1962 Alabama-Georgia game, when he had to suspend quarterback Joe Namath in 1963, and when quarterback Pat Trammell, one of his all-time favorite players, died of cancer at the age of 28.

In talking with many of Bryant's former players, I was touched at just how emotional and transparent he was. He would get teary-eyed over the big games, especially when playing rival Tennessee. And, as we've already heard, emotions were at an all-time high during Liberty Bowl week in 1982, the final one of his long and storied career.

Similar to the way Bryant would often poor-mouth his teams, he frequently poor-mouthed himself, calling himself "just a plow hand from Arkansas," or "no smarter than anybody else." Whether or not he was sincere is not important.

Bryant was fully human and vulnerable, and for that, his players – and the Alabama nation – loved him even more.

Chapter Four

CHARACTER COUNTS

"There are just three things I ever say: If anything goes bad, then I did it. If anything goes semi-good, then we did it. If anything goes real good, then you did it. That's all it takes to get people to win football games for you."
—PAUL W. "BEAR" BRYANT

There has been a great debate in our country for quite a while about this whole issue of leadership and character. Regarding an elected official, one school of thought says if the polls and the economy are good, then character isn't that important. The other argument is that you can't lead without character. There's a real debate, so what's the answer?

One time at a conference, I heard former Oklahoma congressman J.C. Watts ask those in attendance, "How many of you wives think the character of your husband is important?" Not one arm failed to go up.

Then he said, "How many of you husbands think the character of your wife is important?" Again, one hundred percent raised their arm.

"Then don't tell me the character of our leaders is not important!" Watts said. "You can no more have leadership without character than you can have water without the wet."

I think Coach Bryant would agree with that. As motivational speaker and author John Maxwell reminds us, you can only go as high on the leadership ladder as your character will allow you.

What does Coach Bryant teach us about character? Let's find out.

HONESTY & INTEGRITY

Exactly what is honesty? What is integrity?

Motivational expert Spencer Johnson, author of *Who Moved My Cheese?*, says, "Honesty is telling the truth to other people. Integrity is telling myself the truth."

Honesty is telling the unvarnished, unleashed, unmasked truth in every situation. That doesn't mean you have to decapitate people with honesty that buries them. For example, I wouldn't advise telling a co-worker that her makeup looks lousy, even if it does. Or telling the chairman of the board that he needs to shed a few pounds, even if he needs to.

Likewise, a leader with integrity has a consistency to his life; he's the same every day. I've always had the impression that the tongue in Coach Bryant's mouth was pointing in the same direction as the tongue in his shoes; his walk and his talk matched.

Every time you speak, those who work for you, or are around you, must know that they can take your word to the bank. With Bryant, his honesty and integrity were never in question.

"When Coach spoke, we knew it was the truth every time," said Joe Koch, a guard and linebacker under Bryant at Kentucky in 1952-54. "That, to me, is the mark of a great leader. I didn't always want to hear what he was saying, but I knew it was always true."

Steve Bowman, fullback on the 1964 and 1965 Alabama national championship teams, said, "Coach had enormous respect from his players and coaches. How did he get it? We believed him because he was truthful with us. He was a proven winner, so who were we to argue with him? He never asked us to do anything he hadn't already done. He taught us how to act and work hard. We listened to him intently and took it all to heart. He was honest with us; all of us believed in him."

The task of filling Bryant's head coaching shoes at the University of Alabama went to Ray Perkins, a member of two Tide national championship teams and an All-American in 1966. "Coach Bryant was a loyal guy to his players, coaches and the school," Perkins said. "We admired his honesty and integrity and his confidence and poise. He instilled that in us with his presence."

Placekicker Bill Davis, who still holds the Alabama season record for most points-after-touchdowns, said, "Whatever Coach told you, you could bank on it. If he set a rule, he stood by it. If you broke it, it wasn't his fault; it was yours. There had to be a punishment if you stepped over the line. But he cared about his players and if Coach told you he'd help you later in life, he'd do it."

Three-time All-American linebacker Woodrow Lowe, a recent inductee into the College Football Hall of Fame, added, "Coach Bryant had a lot of integrity. He never said anything he didn't mean. He'd never lie to you."

Edwin Pope, long-time sports columnist in Atlanta and Miami, covered Bryant for years. "Bear was an honest guy and a very interesting man," Pope said. "He'd tell me personal things about his players, his family, or other coaches. All those observations didn't always bring great glory to him, but he was just a transparent man.

"Also, Coach was honest enough and willing enough to own up to his mistakes. That's an endearing quality when you admit to your faults."

Fred Sington, Jr., the only Alabama player to have played for Red Drew, J.B. "Ears" Whitworth, *and* Paul Bryant, recalls Bryant's honesty. "In 1959, we beat Houston, 3-0, on my field goal," Sington said. "Coach Bryant told me, 'That's the worst field goal I've ever seen. If you can't do better, we'll have to get someone else.' The next day he apologized and said he'd seen the films and it was a bad snap."

Roy Exum started covering Alabama and SEC football in his early 20s for *The Chattanooga News-Free Press*, his family's newspaper. Bryant was the subject of many of his stories and columns. "Coach was one-of-a-kind," Exum said. "He was larger than life and people instantly believed in him. His entire philosophy was built around the principle of doing things the right way. His honesty was quite evident his entire career."

In covering Bryant for *Sports Illustrated*, Frank Deford, six-time U.S. Sportswriter of the Year, said, "As tough as Bryant was, he was able to get his players to believe and trust in him, which was very important. They liked him and listened to him. Personality was a big part of Bear's success as a leader.

"It's easy to be a leader if all you do is intimidate and browbeat people. There has to be some affection there if you want to get your players to do what you want. Affection has to be blended into the mix and Bryant was able to do that. He couldn't have gotten it out of them if he wasn't honest with them and if they didn't believe in him."

RESPONSIBILITY

Unfortunately, we are living in an age of deflected responsibility. Leaders make decisions and if they work out, they can't wait to take the credit. If they don't work out, many leaders develop a case of "instant amnesia." They have no memory of the situation and then just to make sure, hire a spin-doctor to get them out of the mess they created.

Believe me, Coach Bryant never needed any spin-doctors. He manned up and took total responsibility, on and off the field.

Of those closest to Bryant off the field, no one could vouch for his taking responsibility more than Rebecca Christian, his secretary from the mid-1960s to the early 1980s. "Coach didn't like to bask in the glory of all of his successes," Christian said. "He wanted his players to get the credit. Whenever there was a problem or things weren't going well, he'd take full responsibility for it. I think that's the main reason he had a lot of good people working with him over the years."

Basketball coach Wimp Sanderson spent 32 years on the UA campus, 20 as an assistant coach and 12 as head coach. His many years working under Bryant (as athletic director) taught him many life lessons. "Coach knew how to win," said Sanderson, whom Bryant picked to succeed C.M. Newton as head coach in 1980. "He'd always give credit when it was due and never to himself. He also knew how to lose, although he hated it. He'd give the other team credit and lay the blame on himself."

Former Georgia head football coach Vince Dooley faced Bryant six times, winning twice and losing four. Even as an opposing coach, he has nothing but praise for Bryant. "If Bear made a mistake, he would admit and apologize," Dooley said. "He accepted responsibility for his decisions. So many leaders today are eager to take the credit if things are going well, but they'll push others out front to take the blame if things turn out badly."

Julie Strauss McLaughlin, for many years co-producer of *The Bear Bryant Show*, said, "On his TV show, Coach gave all the credit to his players and took all the blame himself. You'd hear him say things like, 'That was a bad call on my part,' or 'We didn't have a good game plan,' or 'We didn't prepare the team well enough.' Never did he blame the team."

Bill "Brother" Oliver, who played for Bryant at Alabama in 1958-61, coached defensive backs for him in 1971-79, and faced him as an Auburn assistant coach in the late 1960s, said, "Coach was obsessed with being the very best coach possible. I learned he was a genius on both sides of the ball. He did all the substituting, which no head coach does today. When asked why, he said, 'It's my team and I'm not going to let anyone mess it up.' It was his team and he coached it. He took full responsibility for everything that went on."

One of Oliver's finest defensive backs at Alabama was Don McNeal, an unsung hero on the famous "Goal Line Stand" series in the 1979 Sugar Bowl. "Coach made sure we were prepared going into every game," McNeal said. "If you made a mistake, he took responsibility. He'd say, 'That's my fault and I'll fix it.'"

Jim Krapf, an All-American offensive lineman in the early 1970s, said, "Coach would give you responsibility, but with that you knew you were also being held accountable. He'd stick by you as long as you were doing everything possible to help the team. You had to conform to what was best for the team. His rules were absolute, although he'd modify them when necessary. He would never ask you to do anything that wouldn't benefit the team."

Not only did Bryant *take* responsibility, he also *taught* it. Quarterback Joe Namath, in the aftermath of his suspension for the final two games of the 1963 season, learned first-hand from Bryant what it meant to be responsible. "Coach Bryant taught us so many basics of life that continue to hold up today," Namath said. "The main thing was responsibility. It's not easy, but you have to be responsible and learn to do things that are hard.

"When Coach suspended me, it was very hard on him. We were at his home discussing the situation and he just fell back on the bed. I was scared, really scared. I asked if he was okay and he said yes. He sat up and said, 'Well, Joe, I'm going to have to go ahead and suspend you.' He told me to report to his office at 1:00 p.m.

"When I got there, Coach and all his assistants were standing in the foyer," Namath continued. "Coach said, 'My coaches and I had a meeting. Some of them think there's another way to go about this issue. But to me, that's not the right way to go. I'll retire before that.'

"I was so embarrassed and pleaded, 'Coach, don't do that.' He then said, 'We're going to have to move you out of the dorm. If you want to leave Alabama, I'll help find another place for you to go. If you want to stay and do everything the way I want it, you can come back to spring practice.'

"I went back out in the spring and discovered I was listed as the fifth string quarterback. I moved up the charts very gradually. Coach Bryant was teaching me a lesson that stays with me to this day."

HARD WORK

A great leader must have an intense work ethic. There's just no other way around it. If a leader is lazy, then he's not a leader.

Coach Bryant's work ethic was unmatched. He was consumed around the clock with football, football, and more football. "There is no substitute for hard work – none," Bryant once said. "If you work hard, the folks around you are going to work harder. If you drag into work late, what kind of impression is that going to leave on your fellow workers? If you leave early, what kind of impression is that going to leave?"

To put Bryant's work ethic into perspective, and to illustrate his feelings toward cross-state rival Auburn, one phone call sums it up. "…One morning at 7:00 a.m.," Bryant wrote in *Bear*, "I placed a call from my office to Shug Jordan or somebody at Auburn, and the girl said nobody was in yet. I said, 'What's the matter, honey, don't you people take football seriously?' Everybody thought that was a nice joke, but I meant it."

For Bryant to have had so much success in his long career, his work ethic had to trickle down to his coaching staff and players. Dick Mitchell, who played safety and halfback for Bryant at Kentucky, remembers well Bryant's demands.

"Coach Bryant worked us very hard," Mitchell said. "He thought if you practiced for two hours and were good, why not practice for four hours and be twice as good? After his practices, we didn't walk off the field, we crawled.

"Years later at a reunion, I asked Coach, 'Would you still practice like that if you could change?' He said, 'Back then I didn't realize you could go too far. I changed my approach as the years went on.'"

Mitchell recalls one particular time when his Kentucky squad was having *too* good a time. Bryant put a stop to it real fast.

"If you were having too good a time, Coach would get upset," he said. "In 1952, we played the University of Miami during the season down at the Orange Bowl. We were in Coral Gables and just having a great time. We went to the beach; most of us had never seen the ocean before. Coach was not happy. He said, 'You're not down here to go swimming; you're here to beat Miami.'

"So the night before the game, he takes us over to Coral Gables High School and puts us through a full-scale scrimmage under the lights. We had on our white game uniforms with the blue numbers. It had rained and we got mud all over them.

"The next night at the Orange Bowl, the Miami fans were thinking, 'Those poor Kentucky guys don't even have clean uniforms.' We won the game, 29-0, so I guess Coach knew what he was doing."

Howard Schnellenberger, a teammate of Mitchell's at Kentucky, credits Bryant's days at Alabama as one reason for his coach's work ethic. "Coach Bryant started under Frank Thomas and learned how to work," Schnellenberger said. "Those years under Thomas were why his work ethic was so pronounced. He told us, 'Work as hard as I demand of you and you will be successful.' That was the bedrock he built on."

Former Auburn head coach Pat Dye, an assistant under Bryant for nine seasons, takes Bryant's work ethic origins back even further – all the way to Moro Bottom, Arkansas. "Coach Bryant had an unsurpassable work ethic, even into the last decade of his coaching career," Dye said. "This capacity to work came because he was a highly motivated individual. I think it all came from his deprived circumstances growing up in Arkansas, and that drove him."

Delbert Reed, former *Tuscaloosa News* sports editor, said, "Coach was willing to work long and hard to achieve his goals. He was known to arrive at work at 5:30 in the morning. Once, after a poor practice, he told the coaches he wanted them at work early the next day for a meeting, and he didn't give a specific time. Some of the coaches slept in their offices that night to be sure they were on time."

Wayne Atcheson, Alabama's sports information director from 1983-88 and assistant director of TIDE PRIDE (the athletic department's ticket priority program) from 1988-2003, was a graduate assistant in 1964-65 for Charley Thornton in the Sports Information Office. As one who was around the Athletic Department every day, Atcheson learned quickly the work ethic Bryant instilled upon his staff.

"I recall one summer, Coach Bryant was gone for a few days on a trip to California," Atcheson said. "During that time, the number of people involved in the football program besides the players was extremely small. You had an assistant athletic director, eight assistant coaches, a trainer and his graduate assistant, an equipment man, four or five managers and trainers, an academic director, a ticket manager with two assistants, the Bryant Hall dorm director, and three department secretaries.

"With this small number of people, national championships were won. Everybody worked together. It never occurred that we needed more people. Coach Bryant was the leader and we just followed behind.

"Still, when Coach Bryant went on that trip, I remember thinking that even though he is two thousand miles away, people here work the same. There is still no small talk going on in the hall, no laughter, no one relaxing. Goofing off was unheard of. It was the same business-like attitude, as if he was sitting in his office or might walk down the hall at any moment. Nothing changed among the workers even when he was out of town.

"No matter what you were doing," Atcheson continued, "Coach Bryant was so highly revered that you always measured your work and time with him in mind. His command of leadership caused everyone to give their very best. He not only set the standard for leadership in our college football program but for the entire nation.

"For most everyone who was honored to be associated with him, that same work ethic was instilled in you for a lifetime. Thus, more leaders were produced from the leadership standards he demonstrated every day."

Kirk McNair, sports information director in the 1970s, echoes Atcheson's thoughts. "We worked hard because he worked so hard, McNair said. "We weren't afraid of him, but we didn't want to disappoint him. Every day we gave our all, primarily for him."

Marc Tyson, Bryant's only grandson, adds, "He was just a hard-working country boy with a desire to win. During the football season he'd get up at 4:30 a.m. He'd put in unbelievable long hours, so he put a sofa in his office and would take his afternoon naps. He simply outworked people."

Bryant's work ethic was a popular topic among the many interviews conducted for this book. Listen in as his players, whose lives he changed, reminisce.

"Coach Bryant led by example and we observed how he did things every day," said Joe Namath. "He certainly put in the time. He lived in that office eating, thinking, and talking football non-stop. He'd be working long before us and long after we'd left the facility. He was a teacher of life and was instructing us in a basic way to get things done."

Gaylon McCollough, one of Namath's centers from 1962-64, said, "We knew that Coach Bryant worked as hard as anybody. He was a hands-on leader. He was the first coach at the office in the morning and the last one to leave. Then he'd go home and fall asleep in his recliner watching film and trying to figure out a way to help get us better prepared."

Tim Bates, who played linebacker in 1963-65, said, "Coach was willing to put in the same amount of work as he'd ask of his players. He'd work just as hard as you did. You could give him a pile of bricks and a bunch of common laborers and he'd get the Empire State Building built. He might kill some of them along the way, but he'd get it built.

"He was up as early as or earlier than anyone else and he stayed as late as or later than anyone else. If I had run my business like he did his football team, I would have been a lot more successful."

Creed Gilmer, a defensive end in 1963-65, said, "Coach's philosophy was, 'I'm going to work as hard as I can and I expect you to do the same.' If you had that winning heart, he would take winners and make better winners out of them."

Jerry Duncan, hero of the 1966 Orange Bowl victory over Nebraska, said, "Coach Bryant's philosophy of life was to get up every morning and go to work. Do something that'll get you better. Do what you have to do to be a better player and person. Coach led by example. No one outworked him and no one got more done than he did."

Robin Parkhouse, All-American defensive end for the Tide in 1971, credits Bryant's work ethic in making him the man he is today. "We heard Coach say, 'It's not the will to win that matters. Everyone has that. It's the will to prepare to win that matters.' I heard him say that in many different ways over my four years.

"That's what separated him from others. He'd get to the office at 5:30 a.m. every day. He outworked most of the competition and expected that from us. That's all part of me now because I played for him. I'm so grateful now as a 60-year old man."

Bryant's work ethic trickled on down to his team. Not only were the Tide players better prepared mentally than their opponents, but they were better prepared physically. "We played Ohio State in the Sugar Bowl and in the third quarter, one of their linebackers was throwing up in the end zone," said Steve Whitman, a fullback on the 1978 and 1979 national championship squads. "We weren't even sweating yet. We went through things in practice that put us way ahead of the other teams regarding conditioning. When the other team was getting tired in the second half, we knew we had a lot left."

Quarterback Steadman Shealy, a teammate of Whitman's, added, "Coach Bryant expected excellence from himself and from us. He was never satisfied with what he'd just accomplished. I remember when he was getting close to Stagg's record and even then he was not satisfied. He told me he never wanted to go back to plowing. His philosophy was to work hard and get a little better every day."

As mentioned earlier, Bryant was obsessed with football and the work it required, once saying, "48 hours is all that anybody ought to enjoy anything. Then it's time to get back to work."

Sports Illustrated writer John Underwood, who wrote Bryant's auto-biography *Bear*, once asked Bryant his thoughts on retiring. Bryant's chilling answer was, unfortunately for the college football world, prophetically accurate.

"In the late 1960s," Underwood recalls, "I once said to Bryant, 'You've won three titles and gone to the top of your profession. Why don't you retire and enjoy the fruit of your labor?' He said, 'No, if I did that, I'd croak in a week.'

"He died a month after his last game and I thought back to that conversation. Coaching football was everything to him."

PERSEVERANCE

Perseverance is the character quality of hanging in there, sticking with it, and not surrendering.

Yes, there will be times when you're discouraged and feeling down, but a leader must persevere. If you as a leader don't persevere, how can you expect your troops to? If you cave in, what will keep your employees from doing the same?

In the early 1960s, when Alabama football was rapidly on the rise, Bryant was hit with two major accusations – excessive brutality (by Furman Bisher of *The Atlanta Journal-Constitution* via *The Saturday Evening Post*) and, along with Georgia Athletics Director Wally Butts, "fixing" the 1962 Alabama-Georgia game (by *The Saturday Evening Post*).

The game-fixing accusations crushed Bryant, but he had no choice but to persevere. "How much is a year of a man's life worth?" wrote Bryant in *Bear*. "I don't know, but *The Saturday Evening Post* took ten years off my life and I billed them $10 million for it. I guarantee you, if I had collected that much – which I didn't – it would not have paid the suffering they put me through."

Bryant, by practically all accounts, was eventually exonerated on the brutality charges. Regarding the game-fixing accusation, after an emotional trial he settled with Curtis Publishing Company, the parent company of *The Saturday Evening Post*. As hard a time as he went through, though, his perseverance was evident. During the two seasons Bryant was battling these charges, the Tide went 19-3. The three losses were by a total of only seven points.

Not only did Bryant *have* perseverance, but he *taught* it. His favorite expression to his players throughout his career was something like, "If you think it's tough now, just wait…" The illustrations he used were to teach perseverance, and today, his players are thankful for those many life lessons.

"After a practice in training camp," recalls linebacker Darwin Holt, "Coach would say, 'Evidently some of you think it's too tough out here. Some of your buddies have already left and they never even said goodbye. Life is not easy. If you think this is tough, just wait until you get out in the world. Your wife is eight months pregnant, you're behind on your mortgage, and now you have to come home and tell the wife you've lost your job. Your buddies would quit on the wife and baby, but you guys won't.' It was his way of telling us to be tough and stick it out."

Steve Bowman remembers Bryant's constant reminders to hang in there, stick it out, and persevere. "I still hear Coach's voice today," Bowman said, "and he's saying, 'Don't give up. Don't quit. Stay with it. When life gets tough on you, what are you going to do, fold up and quit?' Coach taught us that life is not handed to you. He really instilled that in us."

Ken Wilder, a late 1960s offensive lineman, and Steve Mott, an early 1980s center, recall similar Bryant wisdom, but with real-life consequences. "Coach would tell us that story about coming home and your wife was gone and you'd lost your job," Wilder said. "Well, one time I was away on a fishing trip and when I got back, my company had closed up and I was out of work. I later told Coach about that and he kind of grinned and said, 'I told you life can be hard.'"

Mott shares a similar story. "Coach was famous for that message to us about losing your job, your dog bites you, and your wife runs off," he said. "Well, four years ago, I lost my business in my late forties and had to start all over again. I thought about Coach every day through that ordeal."

Pat Raines, a center on the 1971 SEC championship team, said, "Playing football for Coach Bryant was almost a spiritual experience for me. His one statement still rolls through my mind: 'Being tired makes cowards of us all.' Every day in my life there is something I've got to press through and get done. Those lessons on perseverance from Coach Bryant will stick with me forever."

Wes Neighbors, a redshirted freshman on Bryant's last team, added, "With Coach, it was not just about football. He'd tell us, 'If you make it through four years at Alabama, you'll never quit anything in life. That's a promise.' Alabama football was all about never quitting."

How true. Alabama football was indeed about never quitting. And although Bryant decided during the latter half of the 1982 season to hang it up, for him it was all about *retiring*, not quitting. Paul W. "Bear" Bryant and the word "quit" are, by definition, incompatible.

Linda Knowles, who served as Bryant's secretary during his last season, credits his perseverance for getting through the year. "During Coach's last year, he was a very sick man, and he willed himself to live," Knowles said. "I don't know if he knew how short his time was, but I think he had the drive and will to complete that season and to have things in order before he died."

HUMILITY

We think of a major head football coach as this boisterous, overwhelming, ego-driven character from another age. But in describing this person, we're not describing Coach Bryant.

The more we study Bryant, the more we see that he was understated and quiet. One of the former coaches I interviewed told me that Bryant really didn't like the limelight. If it was forced on him, then he'd deal with it, but he didn't seek it out.

Bryant dined with celebrities, walked with presidents, and for more than 25 years was the most powerful figure in college football. But at the same time, he had a heart for the little guy, for the common man, for the custodian that cleaned his office, for the ticket takers at the stadium, and for that Crimson Tide fan from Smalltown, Alabama, who just wanted a handshake or an autograph. Grambling coach Eddie Robinson once said, "The greatest thing about Coach Bryant was that he could talk to kings and queens and the man in the street."

Former Alabama head coach Gene Stallings, a 2010 inductee in the College Football Hall of Fame, said, "Here's the essence of Coach Bryant in a nutshell – all people wanted to please him; from players to coaches to alumni to the college president. Leadership is a lot easier when everyone wants to please you."

Marc Tyson, in talking about his grandfather's humility, said, "Gene Stallings said it best: 'Coach Bryant had a knack for wanting everyone to please him.' Why did everyone want to please him?

"I believe it was because he was very humble to the common man. He treated everyone fairly, whether they were black or white, young or old. He had time for everyone. He went to Krystal to eat breakfast and then to the catfish place for dinner. People would swarm all over him, but he'd sign autographs and didn't hide from the public."

Winston Groom, a 1965 Alabama graduate and author of *Forrest Gump* and *The Crimson Tide: The Official Illustrated History of Alabama Football,* said, "Coach Bryant will always be beloved in the state of Alabama. He was a humble man, a private person and one who was sparing with his words. You'd watch his Sunday TV show and notice how self-deprecating he was. He took all the blame and gave away all the credit."

Mal Moore played for Bryant from 1958-62, coached with him from 1964-82, and since 1999 has served as athletic director at Alabama. Moore recalls Bryant's humility, especially regarding his wins and losses. "Coach Bryant stressed to all of us lucky enough to be around him that football teaches the principles of life, the peaks and valleys and how to deal with each of them," Moore said.

"When you win, you should be thankful and humble. When you are at rock bottom, don't ever give up, keep fighting, and ultimately, success will come again."

Herschel Nissenson, long-time sportswriter for the Associated Press, covered Bryant for many years and was always impressed by his humility. "At a press conference before the season one year," Nissenson said, "someone asked Bear, 'How do you feel about being ranked number one in the polls?' He said, 'Well, one year we were ranked first before the season, won 'em all, and finished third. So it ain't no big deal.'"

Lanny Norris, a Tide defensive back in the early 1970s, sums up how the Alabama players felt about pleasing Bryant. "When we played on Saturday afternoons," Norris said, "there'd be 60,000 in the stands, including our friends and families. That crowd didn't matter because the only person we cared about pleasing was that man on the sideline with the hat on."

CLASS

You think of Coach Bryant and you think "class." You think of "class" and you think Coach Bryant. The two really can't be separated.

"I don't know what class is, but I can tell you when someone has it," Bryant would say. "You can tell it from a mile away."

Here's another Bryant gem: "I have tried to teach them to show class, to have pride and to display character. I think football – winning games – takes care of itself if you do that."

Bryant *had* class and he *taught* class. "Show your class," he would often say.

Mal Moore, a fixture on the sidelines standing next to Bryant, said, "When we didn't win, Coach Bryant always praised the other team and accepted the blame for the loss. He never pointed his finger at the failings of his coaches or the team. He often said, and emphasized, that you should win with dignity and lose with class. I hope I learned that from him as a player and assistant coach."

Two All-Americans from the 1960s, Lee Roy Jordan and Dennis Homan, share game moments when Bryant preached class to his players.

"A 7-6 loss to Georgia Tech in 1962 kept us from winning consecutive national championships," Jordan said. "Coach Bryant took all the blame for the loss. After two days of feeling sorry for ourselves and having very poor practices, he had all the starters go to the projection room to watch film of the crucial play that should have won the game for us.

"After watching every player miss his block on the play, Coach used one of his patented talks to explain that we could write off the season or we could bounce back and show the kind of class that he knew we had. The next week, we beat Auburn and went on to an impressive victory over Oklahoma in the Orange Bowl."

Throughout the entire 1966 regular season, the Tide defense surrendered only 37 points and recorded five shutouts. A year later, in the 1967 home opener against Florida State, *in just one game*, the defense gave up 37 points. Bryant's halftime speech to his players was filmed by ABC Sports as part of a special documentary hosted by Chris Schenkel.

Homan recalls Bryant's halftime challenge. "At the half, Florida State led us 24-22," Homan said. "Coach Bryant came in and said, 'This just makes it perfect. We're behind and they're all fired up. If we've got class, we're going to find it out. I know we've got it!'

"The game ended in a 37-37 tie and of course we were all frustrated and disappointed. As usual, Coach Bryant started taking the blame for not preparing us adequately.

"He said, 'I contributed nothing from the bench. Maybe the Good Lord is testing us. If He's testing me, I've been here before. We need to forget this one; it's gone. Ten minutes after a game is too late; the next day is too late. We need to use this as a stepping stone. If we've got class, we'll be all right. If we don't, it doesn't matter. Keep your heads up. Act like a champion!' His choice of words and his timing were always perfect."

Fran Curci, head coach at Kentucky from 1973-81, recalls a time when Bryant's class shone brightly. "My first game at Kentucky, we played Alabama," Curci said. "Bear was returning to one of his old coaching spots, so he wore blue to honor Kentucky. At the half, we were up 14-0, so he was a little shaken.

"We kicked off to start the second half and Willie Shelby fumbled and the ball went forward. Somehow he came up with the ball and got by everybody and went all the way to score. We could've been up 21-0, but it was 14-7. Alabama went on to win, 28-14, and after the game Bear came over and was most respectful to all of us. He was always a class act."

Alabama golfer Jerry Pate, winner of the 1976 U.S. Open, learned first-hand Bryant's charge to "show your class." "After I had a lot of success in the fall of my senior year," Pate recalls, "Coach told me one day, 'I want you to go to Birmingham with the team this weekend.' I said, 'What should I wear?' He replied, 'Wear something that's lucky.'

"Then he said, 'I don't care what you wear, but look good, act good, and talk good. You are representing the University of Alabama and you have to look good when you travel with me. Be a gentleman and always act with class.'"

Wilbur Jackson, the first black football player signed by Bryant, said, "We met with Coach Bryant every day for three years. His message was to always carry yourself with class on and off the field. Some guys do that great on the field, but not so great off the field. Coach wanted us to act with class at all times. He was teaching us leadership with that lesson."

I asked many of Bryant's former players if they still heard Coach Bryant's voice today and if so, what he was telling them. To a man, he's telling them to "show your class."

"When I joined the Dolphins, Coach sent me a telegram," said Don McNeal. "It said, 'Always show your class.' I put it in my scrapbook. I'm very proud of that. I still hear his voice telling me, 'Don, show your class wherever you go and whatever you do.'"

Running back Tony Nathan, McNeal's teammate at Alabama and with the Miami Dolphins, added, "I still hear Coach Bryant's voice. He's saying, 'Show your character and class.' We were all young, dumb and high strung, but Coach knew how to deal with us."

Barry Smith, a snapper on the 1978 and 1979 national championship teams, said, "What did I learn from Coach that carries over to this day? If you have poise, confidence and class and never give up, you will always have a chance to win. If you heard that enough from Coach, you believed it."

INFLUENCE

When it comes to Coach Bryant, if there is any trait of leadership of his (besides motivation) that deserves an entire book of its own, this is the one.

Influencing the people under you is really the only way to lead. You can talk leadership and teach leadership, but at the end of the day, you lead by your influence.

I don't think Coach Bryant ever took courses in leadership, or was reading the great leadership philosophers of his day, or was taught it by his parents in Moro Bottom, Arkansas. But, he understood that as a leader, you really lead by influencing others.

Bryant's influence is everywhere and is still felt decades later. Where is Coach Bryant today? He's in his people, in his former players. He's *in* Mal Moore, Lee Roy Jordan, Major Ogilvie, Howard Schnellenberger, and Ken Wilder. He's *in* Victor Turyn, Gene Stallings, Babe Parilli, Rich Wingo, and Kenny Stabler. He's living inside of them and they hear his voice to this day. His lessons have permeated their souls. He's as active and influential in their lives today as he was when they were 20-year olds playing for him.

By the time you soak in the upcoming thoughts and stories, you'll be influenced by Coach Bryant as well. First, let's look at some media perspectives.

"The three most beloved Southerners of all time are Robert E. Lee, Stonewall Jackson, and Bear Bryant, in that order," said ESPN college football analyst Beano Cook. "No one disliked Bryant – the man was something special, and we're still seeing his influence today."

Keith Dunnavant, author of *Coach: The Life of Paul "Bear" Bryant*, makes a convincing case for Bryant's life-long influence in his players' lives. "For a certain type of kid," Dunnavant said, "Bryant could elevate the game of football and make it so important, that that player would be willing to push himself to his outer limits and beyond.

"In other words, football became a metaphor for life. These guys would take his punishment and go through an almost transcendent experience. That allowed them to use football at Alabama as a path to an outstanding life. Playing for Bear Bryant at Alabama became a proving ground to show what you could do out in the world. If you did whatever it took to please him, the long term impact would result in abundant fruit."

Another Bryant biographer is Mickey Herskowitz, author of *The Legend of Bear Bryant*. Herskowitz, who as a 19-year old began covering Bryant's career at Texas A&M, recalls a personal Bryant story of influence. "People wanted to be like him and imitate him," Herskowitz said. "I was with him one day, and we both were battling colds. He pulled out a bottle of cough syrup and took two swigs from the bottle. I took out my bottle and measured out two spoonfuls, very carefully. Bear said, 'What are you doing?' I told him. He said, 'Just drink from the bottle.' And ever since, I have."

Charlie Land, former sports editor and publisher of *The Tuscaloosa News*, said, "One summer, I attended a reunion of the three national championship teams of the 1960s," Land said. "It was interesting sitting around the swimming pool listening to them talk. To a man, they'd tell you that hardly a day would go by that they didn't think of something Coach Bryant had told them over the years. That's a powerful impact."

If any one particular group can claim Bryant's life-long influence, it would most definitely be the 54 of his players or assistant coaches who went on to become head coaches at the college or professional level. Five of them — Howard Schnellenberger, Mike Riley, Neil Callaway, E. J. Junior, and Joey Jones – are active head coaches today. Just imagine the number of players that *those* 54 have influenced through the years, all because of a man named Paul "Bear" Bryant.

We mentioned in Chapter Two how Bryant's ability to motivate his players was a result of his motivation as a youngster. According to Pat Dye, one of those 54 Bryant disciples, the same can be said of Bryant's influence.

"Coach had a knack for searching out great role models," Dye said. "He played for Frank Thomas who learned under Knute Rockne. Then he coached under Red Sanders at Vanderbilt. General Neyland at Tennessee, Bobby Dodd at Georgia Tech, and Jim Tatum at Maryland all had an influence on him. He picked top-notch people in his profession to learn from."

Bobby Bowden never played for Bryant or coached against him, but he revered and idolized him. "Bear got to Alabama in 1958, and I became the head coach at Samford in 1959," said Bowden, who served as Florida State's head coach from 1976-2009. "I copied everything he did regarding coaching approaches. I tried to emulate how he went about the coaching profession. He was my idol."

Lou Holtz, known by today's younger generation as an ESPN commentator more so than a long-time head football coach, was also influenced by Bryant. "I got to know Coach Bryant well," said Holtz, whose Arkansas squad fell to Bryant and Alabama in the 1980 Sugar Bowl. "I learned many things from him. Coach Bryant was the one coach Woody Hayes held in high esteem. The qualities and strengths I learned from Coach Bryant are the things I tried to emulate when I was coaching.

"While at Arkansas, we played Alabama in the 1980 Sugar Bowl with the national championship on the line. At a function where both teams were in attendance, some of our players stood in line to get Coach Bryant's autograph. My son, Kevin, now a lawyer, has one of his most prized possessions – a picture of him, at the age of eight, with Coach Bryant."

Former Alabama head basketball C.M. Newton, who played basketball at Kentucky when Bryant was the Wildcats' head football coach and was hired by Bryant in 1968 as the Tide's head basketball coach, said, "I learned a great deal from Coach Bryant and consider him a tremendous influence in my life.

"I learned so much about coaching by watching him and how he did things. His planning, organizing, and dealing with players was superb. I watched some of his practices and he rehearsed every conceivable situation, with the down and time on the clock. I took that into my basketball coaching and would rehearse a 40-minute game down to the second. I felt that if he could do it for 120 players, I could certainly do it for 15 guys."

As I said earlier, an entire book could be written solely on Coach Bryant's influence on his players. From Maryland (1945), to Kentucky (1946-53), to Texas A&M (1954-57), to his alma mater Alabama (1958-82), the impact Bryant made on his hundreds of players during his 38 years as a head coach is incalculable. And that's not to mention those who worked for him, those who were touched in some way by his generosity, and the tens of thousands of Alabama football fans far and wide. Listen in as players from all four schools remember.

"I served under Coach Bryant at the North Carolina Pre-Flight School during World War II," said Joe Drach, a tackle and defensive end at Maryland. "There were 25 of us who played football for him, then he took all of us with him to the University of Maryland. He altered all of our lives.

"I played in the first college game he ever coached in 1945. I saw his 315th win against Auburn in 1981 and I was at the last game he coached in Memphis in 1982. We had a long chat after that game. He was a magnificent guy and a great coach. We stayed friends his whole life."

Ed Schwarz, a guard at Maryland, adds, "I'm almost 90 years old and I think about Coach Bryant to this day and how good he made you feel about yourself and how important you felt as part of his team."

Jim Proffitt, an end for Bryant at Kentucky in 1951-53, said, "Coach never asked you to do something that he wasn't willing to do himself. He led by example. Some people hold back and others get out front. He was always out front. He just had the attitude about him that made you want to follow wherever he was going. The lessons he taught have stayed with us all these years."

Lou Karibo, another one of Bryant's Wildcat players, said, "When Coach sat down at the dinner table, he never had to ask for anything. All he had to do was look at the salt and pepper and people would start passing it to him."

Jack Pardee, one of Bryant's famed "Junction Boys" at Texas A&M, gives thanks to Bryant for his entire football career. "Coach Bryant had a big influence in my life," said Pardee, a 17-year NFL veteran and former head coach of the Chicago Bears, Washington Redskins, and Houston Oilers. "Early in life I set a goal to be a coach and Coach Bryant inspired me to go for it."

Marvin Tate, a teammate of Pardee's at Texas A&M and Aggie athletic director in 1978-81, recalls a humorous story illustrating Bryant's long shadow. "In 1982, Coach Bryant was honored at a dinner in Washington, D.C. and a bunch of us went up from Texas

A&M," Tate said. "I had just lost my job as A&M athletic director. About that same time, I had grown a mustache. I told my wife, 'Coach won't like this mustache.'

"We checked into the Washington Hilton Hotel and set up for a party in our suite. The phone rang and it was Coach inviting us up to visit him in his suite. We got on the elevator carrying our drinks, but on the way to his suite, all the drinks ended up on the hallway floor or in a potted plant. None of us wanted Coach to see us with a drink in our hands.

"We all lined up to greet him and I was last in line. Coach put his arm around me and asked, 'Are you alright?' He was concerned about my job loss. Then he added, 'I hardly recognized you with that mustache.'"

From Bryant's former players at Alabama, here are a handful of testimonies and stories citing Bryant's influence.

"Coach has impacted my life and still does today," said Scooter Dyess, a member of Bryant's first two Alabama teams in 1958-59. "As the years go on, I appreciate him more and more. It's amazing to me that I got to play for the greatest college football coach of all time."

Darwin Holt, a transfer to Alabama from Texas A&M and a member of the 1961 national championship team, has similar feelings. "I think about Coach Bryant every day," Holt said. "All of his players do. He speaks to me as well. I hear him say, 'I told you it was going to be tough. Suck it up. Life's not easy. You've got to keep going!'

"You have to be emotionally connected to a leader like that or you couldn't do what he demanded. Playing for him was not easy. It was not for everyone. Some left, but only the quitters have a bad word about him. Those who stayed had their lives impacted forever."

Bud Moore, also a member of Bryant's first national championship squad in 1961, said, "Coach Bryant was a big man and everything he did was big. His influence to this day is big. I still dream about him at night and I hear his voice to this day. He's saying, 'You've got to be positive.'

"Coach coached football but he taught us about life. Before practice he'd say, 'This is the first day of the rest of your life. Let go of what happened yesterday.' He impacted a lot of us."

Jimmy Sharpe, yet another one of Bryant's pupils to become a head coach, added, "All of Coach Bryant's lessons to us were about being prepared for life after football. It was always about succeeding in life. You had to pay the price now to gain success later. It wasn't just about football, but the rest of your life. He was always talking about life and what it took to be successful."

Lee Roy Jordan, a member of the college and pro football halls of fame, said, "All of us are so proud that Coach Bryant is a part of our lives. It's almost impossible to express how much he meant to us and how he shaped our lives."

Joe Namath, to this day the most recognizable Crimson Tide football player in history (other than Bryant himself), believes Bryant's upbringing influenced his players as much as anything. "As a leader, Coach Bryant's life experiences are what convinced us to follow him," Namath said. "As we learned about his tough background, we realized his plans were a lot more astute than the plans of us young guys. We knew life had been hard for him and he had to work from the get-go.

"The man knew how life worked. His message was: 'Life is hard; you've got to do hard things, whether you like it or not.' He stressed that it takes effort to be successful. As young athletes, we thought we knew it all, but still we took his word for it. I have two daughters, ages 24 and 19, and I can relate a whole lot better now as to what Coach Bryant was telling us."

Jimmy Fuller, one of those "little" mid-1960s players, is another of the 54 players or coaches who became a head coach. "Not many days go by that I don't have someone ask me about Coach Bryant," said Fuller, former head coach at Jacksonville State and an assistant at Alabama from 1984-96. "I still dream about him all the time."

Bobby Johns, a two-time All-American defensive back in 1966-67, said, "Coach Bryant made an impact on all of us. When I went into coaching, someone asked me what kind of coach I'd be. I said, 'I'm going to coach like Coach Bryant. That's pretty much all I know.' When Coach passed away, coaching never seemed the same to me."

Ken Wilder, a late 1960s lineman, said of Coach Bryant, "The man had a great impact on all of us. He was tough on us but positive. When you finished your time at Alabama, you were his. Whenever you had to call him, you were never put on hold. You'd get straight through."

Scott Hunter, whose 484 passing yards versus Auburn in 1969 remains a school record, added, "Coach Bryant's picture hangs on my wall with his arm around me telling me something important that could help us win the game."

George Pugh and Ricky Davis were teammates in the early and mid-1970s. Both wear 1973 national championship rings and both have been profoundly influenced by Bryant.

"I played for the best coach ever," said Pugh, now an assistant coach for former Alabama head coach Bill Curry at Georgia State. "There are very few icons in athletics, but Coach Bryant is one of them. The discipline he instilled in me has enabled me to be who I am today. He moved and shaped all of us – players, coaches, cooks, professors, janitors.

"Now, all of us want to pass it on to others. Coach taught us how to be givers and give back to our communities. Be a winner and a giver

– that was his philosophy of life. Not one former player has a negative thing to say about Coach and that's unheard of. All of us were blessed to be in his presence. What a great legacy he has left."

Davis tells a quiet but revealing story of Bryant's influence years after his playing days were over. "I had spent more time around Coach after I finished playing than I had during my four years in school," Davis said. "I worked out in Tuscaloosa for several years while I was playing in the NFL and I would stop and talk with him. He also came to Tampa some while I was playing there and I would visit with him.

"On the afternoon he announced he was retiring (December 15, 1982), I wrote Coach a note and thanked him for what he meant to me, the impact he had on my life, and the lessons he had taught me and every other player who had played for him.

"Several days later, I received a letter back from him that looked like he had typed himself. He said he and Mary Harmon were the ones that wanted to thank me for sharing four years of my life with them. With all that was going on around his retirement, he took the time to write me. I can't tell you how much that meant to me then, and how much it means today."

For Mike Tucker, a Tide defensive back in 1975-77, Bryant's influence started at a young age and continues to this day. "At age five, I started dreaming about playing football for Coach Bryant and the University of Alabama," Tucker said. "All that I have today goes back to him and my time at Alabama. His intense desire for success still motivates us to this day.

"If I could influence my children as deeply as Coach Bryant influenced me, I'd be fine with that."

Marty Lyons, an All-American defensive tackle in 1978, said, "As I look back at Coach Bryant's influence, we were listening to a man who accomplished so much, but never stopped teaching life principles. I didn't really appreciate that until many years later.

"When I was with the Jets, before every season I would get a telegram from him. It said, 'Best of luck. Show your class.' Those words really hit home."

David Hannah, who along with Lyons was an integral part of the famous "Goal Line Stand" series against Penn State in the 1979 Sugar Bowl, coaches at Briarwood High School in Birmingham. Some 30 years later, memories of Bryant still resonate with him.

"Even today on the high school football field, Coach Bryant goes with me every day," said Hannah, the fifth of five Hannahs who played at Alabama. "His lessons and sayings are always with me: 'Expect the unexpected; be prepared every day; keep your poise; play with confidence and class; it takes personal sacrifice to be successful."

For Byron Braggs, yet another of the "Goal Line Stand" heroes, Bryant's lessons were life-changing. "On the last day of your last practice, you'd walk off the field and you'd start remembering all Coach said," Braggs said. "You were almost in tears thinking about the impact Coach had had on your life. The more we've matured, the more his teachings have rung true. It's like a seed planted in your head and as it starts to germinate, it makes more and more sense."

All-American Tommy Wilcox illustrates how Bryant still occupies his thoughts on a regular basis. "I still have dreams about Coach Bryant," said Wilcox, who served as a pallbearer at Bryant's funeral. "You could never be late to a meeting of his. In fact, you'd better be 15 minutes early because he might start early. Even to this day, I dream that I'm late to a meeting or practice. It wakes me out of a dead sleep and then I'm relieved it was only a dream."

Offensive lineman Mike McQueen, another of Bryant's pallbearers, said, "Take a look at all the great leaders who Coach developed.

Just see who he has influenced in sports, education, medicine, law, and so many other fields. It's amazing, but it's really the biblical message about duplication and passing it down to the next generation.

"Coach wanted others to outdistance him. He did all he could to help them and was very proud of their success."

And finally, John Croyle, a new hero of mine (after listening to his Big Oak Ranch stories), puts Bryant and his influence into perspective. "Coach knew who he was and what he was," Croyle said. "Think about the ripple effect of his leadership and the thousands of lives he touches even today.

"He's been gone now 27 years and you are writing a book about him as a leader. That's quite a statement right there about his impact."

Chapter Five

COMPETENCE

"I'm just a plow hand from Arkansas, but I have learned over the years how to hold a team together – how to lift some men up, how to calm down others, until finally they've got one heartbeat, together, a team."
—PAUL W. "BEAR" BRYANT

"You can improve as a leader, but you either have it or you don't. Being a leader in your church might be one thing, but to lead in the world of college or pro sports is something entirely different. Very few can do that."
—GENE STALLINGS

L eaders are good at what they do, which begs the question: How did they get that way? Were they born that way or were they developed?

I look every day in the Orlando paper for a story and headline that says, "Great natural leader born yesterday at Winter Park Hospital." Well, I haven't seen that headline yet, so I've come to the stark reality that leaders can be developed.

I'm sure there are a handful of leaders who come out of the womb ready to lead without any training or background, but very, very few. So, I'm convinced that leadership skills can be developed and enhanced. We can all be better leaders. If we couldn't, why all these seminars, retreats and all these books that are flooding the market today? Why bother writing this book? And why are you reading it?

Coach Bryant wasn't born with the complete leadership package, but he sure learned how to do it. If they had given stars for competency, Coach Bryant would've been a five-star general, wearing them on his hounds tooth hat. If Oscars had been awarded for being competent in all phases of college football, there'd be an entire display of them on hand at the Bryant Museum.

What are some of these competencies that made Bryant such a great football coach? What can we learn from him? After reading this chapter, don't be surprised if you take a few of them to work with you tomorrow.

SOLVING PROBLEMS

Former U.S. Secretary of State Colin Powell put it this way: "Leadership is solving problems. When people stop bringing you their problems, you're through as a leader."

Not a day went by that Bryant wasn't solving some kind of problem, both on the field and off the field. On the field, it could've been how to stop an opponent's inside trap or how to utilize the wishbone offense's passing options against a defense determined to stop the run. Off the field, it could've been related to academics, or the athletic dorm, or disciplinary issues.

One thing's for sure – Bryant tackled all problems head on and was quick to find solutions.

Scooter Dyess credits Bryant's use of his staff to confront the issues. "It's hard to define 'it', but whatever 'it' is, Coach had it," Dyess said. "He had the ability to organize a staff and then get them to pull together, from the lowest to the highest. He'd get the whole crowd pulling in one direction.

"People followed him because they knew he knew what he was doing. Coach would push and pull you to get on the same wavelength. He was good at listening to his assistants and staff and then coming up with a solution to whatever problem there was."

SELLING

Even if you're in "management," you must be a non-stop sales person. If you're not selling your product or idea or initiative to make your company or school or National Guard unit better, then you're not doing your job as a leader.

Don't leave it up to your sales people to sell; you must be involved in what they're doing. I'm not saying you should hit the pavement or man the phones making cold sales calls, but you need to be able to sell to them the *importance* of making those calls. Sell, sell, sell!

I guarantee you that Coach Bryant could sell. He was selling to his recruits the University of Alabama and Crimson Tide football. Short-term, to his players he was selling game plans every week. Long-term, he was selling to them a philosophy, a work ethic, a purpose.

Bryant said it best. "I believe a football player who comes here and stays four years is going to be better prepared to take his place in society and better prepared for life because I think he'll learn some lessons that are very difficult to teach in the home, in the church, or in the classroom. I think that by learning these lessons, he'll win."

My goodness, Coach, where do I sign? Can you imagine having the great Bear Bryant in your house on a recruiting visit? Jeff Rouzie recalls his experience.

"I grew up in Jacksonville, Florida, and was a Gator through and through," said Rouzie, who not only played for Bryant in the early 1970s, but also coached for him from 1976-81. "I went to every Florida home game and thought Florida all the time. When recruiting time came, I got a call from Coach Bryant and I thought it was a joke. I heard that deep voice over the phone and all I could say was, 'Yes sir, yes sir.'

"When he came to visit my house, the whole neighborhood showed up to see him. He was a man's man and looked like John Wayne – tough but fair. I didn't commit to Alabama that night, but I did later when he called me. Coach said, "Jeff, I need to know whether I can count on you for the next four years.' I said, 'Yes sir.' That's all I ever said to him."

Keith Jackson, the voice of college football for four decades, marvels at Bryant's marketing skills. "He was the best marketing coach I ever met," Jackson said. "He knew how to sell a product, from Golden Flake potato chips to Coca-Colas to his football program. He sold to the media, fans, alumni, his players, and especially to Mama while he was recruiting her son.

"If he could get into Mama's kitchen for a piece of pie and some milk, he'd sell her and get her son to Alabama."

Former Tide player Bill Battle, who through the years has been responsible for officially marketing the Bryant name through his Collegiate Licensing Company, took note of Bryant's selling magic. "Coach would work the press to do what he wanted. He'd call them, ask their advice, and then get them turned around to how he was thinking.

"He could get people to buy into his philosophy and take great pride in it. He'd take average players and make them think they were really good."

LEARNING & TEACHING

Vince Lombardi said a long time ago, "They call it 'coaching,' but it's really 'teaching.'"

John Wooden, about whom I have written two books, never used the word "coach." It was always "teach," "teacher," and "teaching."

In order to be a great teacher, you must be a life-long learner. You can't teach unless you're committed to being a learner. And the reason you must learn is because the world is changing so fast. You must be on the cutting edge of learning or you'll be left in the dust of history.

Bryant was a learner; he soaked up football like a sponge. He was always learning so he could teach in the best way possible. "I'm no innovator," Bryant once said. "If anything, I'm a stealer, or borrower. I've stolen or borrowed from more people than you can shake a stick at."

People scoff at this notion, but it's really true. As Pat Dye mentioned in Chapter Four, Bryant learned the game from the best. He was in awe of Alabama coach Wallace Wade, although he never played for him. He learned Xs and Os and how to make game adjustments from his college coach, Frank Thomas, who had learned from the great Knute Rockne. He idolized Oklahoma's Bud Wilkinson, from whom he learned how to be a gracious loser after Wilkinson's congratulatory visit to Bryant's victorious Kentucky locker room following the 1951 Sugar Bowl.

Whether Bryant "stole" something, enhanced it, or invented it, he was, nevertheless, ahead of his time in many areas. Examples include his frequent use of game films in the early 1950s, the implementation of what would eventually be called the shotgun formation (to protect his Kentucky quarterback Babe Parilli), his off-campus boot camps, building an athletic dorm at Alabama, the tackle eligible play, and the enhancement of the wishbone offense in the 1970s.

Bryant is even credited with coining the term "war babies," according to Mickey Herskowitz, author of *The Legend of Bear Bryant*. "Bryant used that term before it became fashionable among social behaviorists," Herskowitz wrote. "It had nothing to do with the baby boomers, those born just after the war. His reference was to the boys who were without a father's hand, firm or otherwise, during the critical pre-teen years (while their fathers were in the war).

"But another message came across. At a key point in their lives, they may have been deprived of discipline. And now Paul W. Bryant was going to supply some. In fact, it was going to be a case of overcompensation."

Let's see how Bryant turned his life of learning into a life of teaching.

"Coach Bryant was a disciplinarian and a real fundamentalist – really the only true fundamentalist I ever had in my life," said Harry Bonk, Bryant's fullback at Maryland. "Of course, that's what made him successful. He believed in what he was doing and if you'd go down that track with him, you'd be successful as well.

"Coach was an inspiration and motivator and as young men he fit into our lives perfectly. He was just right for us. Some days, he was so tough you hated him and thought, 'I will never come back out here.' But the next day, you loved him and were right back out there. He taught us a lot and it was much more than just football."

Babe Parilli, Bryant's All-American signal caller at Kentucky, said, "The secret to Bryant's success was repetition. We did it over and over until the game was a second nature to us. He'd work on your weaknesses until you made the right progress."

Dee Powell, who played for Bryant at Texas A&M and coached for him at Alabama for 20 seasons, said, "I've been in the Air Force and all over the place for decades, but Coach Bryant was the best leader I

ever had. He was honest, tough, and he taught us how to be successful.
He taught us how to pay the price. Coach made us earn it and he was
great at it."

Ken Meyer holds a distinction matched by no one, playing for
legendary coach Woody Hayes at Denison University in Granville,
Ohio, and coaching at Alabama for Bryant. Meyer points out the
teaching strengths of both men.

"Coach Hayes and Coach Bryant were both great disciplinarians
and paid constant attention to all the little details," said Meyer, an
Alabama assistant from 1963-67. "They were good talent evaluators
and great teachers of the game. They knew how to put the round pegs
in the round holes and the square pegs in the square holes."

On the Alabama coaching staff with Meyer was Jack Rutledge, a
member of the Tide's 1961 national championship team. To Rutledge,
Bryant's teaching was life-changing. "Coach Bryant walked with
the highest people in the land for many years, but at heart, he was a
teacher," Rutledge said. "In the latter part of his life, he wasn't talking
about winning football games as much as about life itself.

"I remember when he would stand at the blackboard in front of
his players. He'd draw columns of their stages of life – 0 to 6, 6 to
12, and 12 to 18. Then he would teach life principles regarding these
different stages of life.

"He said that it made no difference whether you were a bricklayer,
truck driver, football coach, preacher, janitor, banker, doctor, or lawyer.
As long as you were happy and a good citizen, you were a success."

Former Tide quarterback and baseball star Butch Hobson echoes
Rutledge's observations. "At heart, Coach Bryant was a teacher," said
Hobson, a mid-1970s star for the Boston Red Sox and later its major
league manager. "He was really teaching us about life after football."

Bobby Smith, one of Bryant's first quarterbacks at Alabama, said, "Coach taught us three life lessons that I've used for all of these years: First, have a plan for everything. Second, work hard. And third, never ever give up."

Lee Roy Jordan, one of the greatest linebackers in college football history, echoes our previous mention of Bryant's learning and its link to teaching. "Coach Bryant was always extremely prepared," Jordan said. "Whenever he was teaching us, he had all his information together and he could get it across to all of us. Whatever he was focused on that day, he was well versed on the topic.

"Many years later, I still ask myself, 'Okay, am I really paying attention to all of those life principles Coach Bryant taught us? Am I doing the right things? Am I associating with the right people?'"

Danny Ford, who played end for the Tide from 1967-69, says Bryant's teaching paid dividends once he was in the coaching profession. "When I became a head coach," Ford said, "I would ask myself, 'What would Coach Bryant do in this situation?' No one could be like him, but all of us coaches remembered what he taught us. During my coaching days, there wasn't a day that went by that I didn't think about something he had taught me."

Jim Krapf, a multi-purpose All-American lineman for the Tide in 1972, recalls Bryant's unique style of teaching. "Coach was a teacher, but we didn't know we were being instructed," said Krapf, who was also a three-time SEC heavyweight wrestling champion. "He was brilliant in that regard; a genius. He knew how to create an environment that produced learning."

George Pugh was among the first black players to attend Alabama, coming in as a freshman in 1972. He, too, credits Bryant as a life-long teaching influence. "When Coach recruited me out of Montgomery, Alabama, he told my parents, 'I'm going to take George and he'll be a better man when I return him to you,'" said Pugh, now a Georgia State assistant coach. "He was right. As a long-time football coach, all my decisions and teachings come from him. Everything I've taught my players and children come from his lessons of the mid-1970s."

Duke head coach David Cutcliffe, a student assistant coach for Bryant in the mid-1970s, said, "Coach Bryant taught winning *all* the time, not some of the time. He was always teaching us the things that made people win. He taught us the importance of taking care of the little things."

Allen Crumbley, E.J. Junior, David Hannah, Jim Bunch, and Dwight Stephenson, teammates in the late 1970s, share similar stories of Bryant's teaching and how it has stayed with them to this day.

"Despite that rough exterior," Crumbley said, "Coach let you know that he cared. That's where it all starts as a leader. He always talked to us about life; football was just his classroom to teach us. I've been in the real estate business in the Tampa area for many years with my Alabama teammate Dewey Mitchell. Coach impacts us to this day because he taught us the importance of daily preparation. He also stressed that if you take control of your attitude and effort, you'll do well and come out on top most of the time."

Junior affirms Crumbley's thoughts. "Everything Coach Bryant taught us on the football field was designed to teach us and prepare us for all the adventures of life that were out in front of us," Junior said. "All the football lessons were connected to life. I use the same method today in my coaching."

In our first chapter, we analyzed Bryant's vision, which I believe is the first quality of a great leader. David Hannah, in his thoughts on Bryant's teaching abilities, calls them "dreams." "I came to the University of Alabama with all sorts of hope and dreams," Hannah said. "I wanted to be part of that great football tradition and be there to win a couple of championships. Coach Bryant taught us not just to dream but also to discipline ourselves in order to achieve those dreams.

"He taught us how to work because that was the key to achieving our goals. His approach allowed us to have success, which stoked our desire to work even harder. You can see how this cycle kept going and produced so much fruit. If not for his teaching us how to work, we wouldn't have been as successful."

Bunch, an All-American offensive tackle in 1979, adds, "Coach would give us so much advice every day. He'd read from Ann Landers' columns trying to make us better each day as players and people. He knew we'd have to go through hard times and he wanted us to possess strength for the future."

Stephenson, an All-American center in 1979 and a member of the Pro Football Hall of Fame, said, "Coach Bryant was always trying to help us as individuals. He wanted us to be successful as adults.

"I played for Don Shula at the Dolphins and he was the same way. Both of these legendary coaches were teaching us life lessons because they cared about us and wanted us to be good people."

Finally, regarding Bryant's teaching ability, let's hear this nugget from Keith Jackson. "One thing I've observed about the great football coaches," he said, "is that they are patient and they are very good teachers. And they could teach under pressure.

"After watching college football for 50 years, I'm convinced you couldn't be a great coach without being a great teacher. Ol' Bear could teach with the best of them."

TEAM BUILDER

In your company, or your church, or your local bowling league, you must take the stray and unaligned parts and pull them together to form a team. The old adage "a chain is only as strong as its weakest link" is appropriate in this case.

"Most big games are won on five to seven crucial plays," Bryant once said. "The team that makes the big plays wins the game. Lay it on the line on every play. You never know which play is the big play. Try to win on this play. When you get eleven people trying to win on every play, you'll win."

Looking back over Bryant's career, he was a team builder. In his quote at the beginning of this chapter, Bryant mentions "one heartbeat, together, a team." From Moro Bottom, Arkansas, to Tuscaloosa, Alabama, and all parts in between, Bryant learned teamwork, taught it, and built his reputation around it.

"Coach Bryant had a plan for himself," said Creed Gilmer, a member of the Tide's 1964 and 1965 national championship teams. "I heard it and it was, 'Follow me. This is our goal but we have to get there as a team. The price of victory is high, but so are the rewards. A lot of you won't make it because you aren't willing to pay the price. If you win, there'll be enough glory for all of you. All of you must contribute to the heartbeat of the team.'"

Of all the player suspensions in Alabama football history, those of Joe Namath in late-season 1963 and Kenny Stabler in spring 1967 are undoubtedly the most famous. Despite having to go through the embarrassment of being suspended, Stabler credits Bryant with turning his life around.

"When I first got to Alabama, I hung on every word Coach Bryant said, but I got away from that and made some bad decisions," said Stabler, who quarterbacked the Crimson Tide to a 28-3-2 record from

1965-67. "Looking back, Coach saved me. He suspended me and stressed to me that no one is expendable. He taught me to be part of the group; it's the only way you'll succeed.

"I can still hear his voice today: 'You must sacrifice and persevere and if you do, you can do anything you want to do.' Coach saw something good in me and saved me from myself. He allowed me to be part of his football family, but only if I would conform to his rules and always put the team first."

Jim Krapf adds, "As long as you gave your best effort, Coach would stick with you. But the minute he sensed you didn't care about the team and were looking for the easy way out, you wouldn't be around very long. He couldn't tolerate selfish players."

Johnny Musso, the workhorse in Alabama's inaugural wishbone offense in 1971, said, "Coach Bryant was such a great team builder because everyone wanted to please him. He encouraged camaraderie among the team. Just surviving forced us to stay together as a team, which helped us build our character.

"Coach's emphasis on team has helped me all my life. He taught me that things worthwhile would be hard to obtain and that nothing would be given to you. He showed me that you couldn't accomplish things on your own, that you needed to work within the framework of others. This team approach applies to everyday life – your marriage, raising kids, your job, whatever."

Steve Ford, defensive back from 1972-74, shares a revealing look into Bryant and his team concept. "Coach Bryant was great at having his players play as a team and buy into the unity concept," said Ford, whose older brother Mike was a Tide All-SEC defensive end in 1968. "We were not all the best athletes, but we could all play a role and fill a spot on the team.

"Coach was good with Xs and Os, but his real strength as a leader was putting a team together. The sum of all his individual talent was far greater than our individual talent alone."

Linebacker Jack Smalley, whose father Jack, Sr. played for the Tide in the early 1950s, said, "Coach insisted that we all had to be on the same page. You had to buy in or you were gone. We all pushed each other because it was never about ourselves.

"We all had a responsibility to the team. When the ball was snapped, all eleven guys wanted to make the tackle. We wanted to win every practice and win every drill, even when no one was watching. If you didn't have a sense of team, you were dead weight."

A linebacker teammate of Smalley's was Barry Krauss, one of the many heroic warriors on the famous "Goal Line Stand" series in the 1979 Sugar Bowl. Krauss recalls two of Bryant's important demands. "There was a price to pay if you were at Alabama," Krauss said. "First was the incredible work ethic it took; and second, you had to be a team player. Coach Bryant wanted you to play for him, but he didn't need you if you put yourself ahead of the team."

Placekicker Peter Kim adds, "Coach Bryant extracted the best out of each player to make it work for the team's success. He didn't always play the best talent, but he used the players who made the whole unit perform better."

Eddie Lowe, younger brother of All-American Woodrow Lowe, played linebacker for the Tide in 1980-82. Lowe has taken Bryant's concepts of "team first" and applies it in his everyday life as a banker.

"The number one thing I learned from Coach Bryant was not to be jealous," Lowe said. "At Alabama, it was all about the team and the people around you. I think you can teach people that and make an organization even stronger.

"I try to do that in my job. It's important to lift people up and be happy for each other when someone does well. I'm constantly teaching people that it's not about you. I tell them if you make those around you look good, you will look good. It thrills me to see people do well and go past me in their careers.

"That's what I learned under Coach Bryant. If each person avoided jealously and was happy with others' successes, it would help the team, the school, the town, and the state."

Bryant's teamwork philosophy extended far beyond the football field, all the way to the WAPI television studios in Birmingham, where the filming of *The Bear Bryant Show* took place. From 4-5 p.m. every Sunday afternoon, viewers tuned in to Bryant's folksy commentary on the previous day's game. Along with co-host Charley Thornton, a bag of Golden Flake potato chips, and a bottle or two of ice cold Coca-Cola, Bryant held captive an entire state.

For a 10-year period in the 1970s, the show was produced by three 20-something women from the Frank Taylor Advertising Agency. One of them, Julie Strauss McLaughlin, recalls Bryant's inclusion of them on his team.

"Coach Bryant was a great team-builder right on our show," McLaughlin said. "He knew our names and we were just three young women who were not important in his world. But he made us feel important and an important part of his team. We'd have suited up and played if he'd asked us to; he was that charismatic. We respected him and trusted him and were very proud to be part of his team."

ORGANIZATION & PREPARATION

The best leaders are those who are organized and prepared. I've noticed this with great coaches such as John Wooden, Vince Lombardi, Dean Smith, and of course, Coach Bryant. Everything was outlined; every practice was extremely organized. There was not one wasted second on the field or on the floor. Practices were run crisply and precisely, and all the players were involved.

Dave Sington, Bryant's first team captain (alongside quarterback Bobby Smith), learned first-hand Bryant's organizational skills during their first spring practice in 1958. For Sington, who had suffered for three years through the short-lived J.B. "Ears" Whitworth era, it was a stark difference.

"Coach Bryant was the most organized person I've ever seen," said Sington, whose father Fred, Sr. was a Tide All-American in 1930 and whose brother Fred, Jr. was a teammate of his in 1958. "He knew the business thoroughly and how to run a practice. He once told me that for every minute of practice, his coaches spent ten minutes planning.

"It didn't take me long to see the obvious differences in coaching philosophies between Whitworth and Bryant. Under Whitworth, we'd go full speed for four or five hours, but not get anything accomplished. Under Bryant, we'd practice two hours and fifteen minutes and accomplish so much more.

"Physically, it was no tougher under Bryant than under Whitworth. But mentally, it was a million times tougher. He just instilled into us not to make errors and to give it one hundred percent all the time."

Jack Rutledge adds, "Coach was a stickler for preparation. He ran a precise practice schedule with everything down to the minute. When you wrote Xs and Os on the blackboard, you'd better have them perfect because he noticed.

"Coach would have the game played before we even left for the stadium on Saturday. He was even prepared for post-game interviews. He had three legal pads ready – what to say if we won, what to say if we tied, and what to say if we lost."

Bill Battle echoes Rutledge's thoughts. "Coach Bryant always had a plan, whether we were ahead by 35 points or behind by 35," Battle said. "The amount of preparation Coach and his staff put in was incredible. They worked all the time. During the games we'd hear the other team's players say, 'You know our plays before we called them.'"

Tommy Brooker, a tight end and placekicker on Bryant's first national championship team in 1961, said, "Coach Bryant was extremely well-organized. His practices were systematically put together and everything scheduled was down on paper. We were always on time and the assistants were all attuned with us. Coach had a big watch and we always went by it. No one was ever idle during practice. We were all moving and rotating in and out of scrimmages."

Lee Roy Jordan, who played for two of the best coaches in the history of football – Paul Bryant of Alabama and Tom Landry of the Dallas Cowboys — shares his thoughts on the two. "The common trait Coach Bryant and Coach Landry possessed was their organizational skills and thorough preparation," Jordan said. "They were always focused on how to improve their teams and get the players to think better. As a result, we *wanted* to do what they were teaching, but not because they demanded it."

In preparing for an upcoming opponent, Bryant never wasted a moment of precious time. "Coach Bryant was very meticulous in his planning, practice schedules, and use of time," said All-American quarterback Steve Sloan, who would later serve as Alabama's athletic director from 1987-89. "He would start preparing at his Sunday meetings and carry it right up to the kickoff on Saturday."

Scott Hunter, record-setting quarterback in the late 1960s, took Bryant's planning and organizational skills and applied them to his own performance. "Coach Bryant was always consistent in what he said and did with me," Hunter said. "He always had a plan and stuck to it and he expected me to do the same. I tried to play quarterback like he coached, with careful attention to details and minimizing mistakes. This helped me even more in the NFL as his approach worked even better up there."

Glenn Woodruff, tight end in 1969-71 and a graduate assistant coach in 1972-73, recalls Bryant's preparation and a saying of his that has lasted forever. "Coach always had a saying, 'Expect the unexpected,'" Woodruff said. "That's how he prepared us. Coach was a preparation guy. What he really did was coach the coaches. He'd tell them, 'Don't expect the players to be ready to play if you're not.' You'd hear him say, 'Don't wait for Saturday to have your plan. Check your plans. What are you going to do?'"

John Mitchell, Tide All-American and currently assistant head coach of the Pittsburgh Steelers, shares how Bryant's tutelage 40 years ago still influences his coaching today. "Everything I learned from Coach Bryant, I practice today," Mitchell said. "Coach would tell us, 'Football is just like taking a chemistry exam. If you're not prepared, you're going to fail. So in the football game, the guy across from you is beating you up, you've got sweat pouring down your face – what are you going to do? I've put you in position during practice to be prepared so you won't quit. I want to see what you'll do *before* Saturday, not *on* Saturday.'"

Randy Scott, a linebacker on Alabama's 1978 and 1979 national championship squads, recalls a time when Bryant's organization paid off handsomely. "Coach Bryant had such organized practices that when I went to play for Green Bay, their detailed practice schedule was easy for me," said Scott, who played for the Packers from 1981-86. "Some of the other rookies' heads were spinning from everyone going in different directions at different times."

Bryant's organizational skills didn't go unnoticed among the state's media. *Huntsville Times* sports editor John Pruett, who covered Bryant for many years, observed, "Coach Bryant was more organized than any other coach at that time. He left nothing to chance and always had a plan for everything. He was way ahead of his time on that.

"His practices were open to the media in those days. I noticed how carefully organized they were. Drills would run no longer than 10-15 minutes, and then the players would sprint to the next station. The whole thing ran like clockwork."

Allen Barra, author of the Bryant biography *The Last Coach*, points out Bryant's mastery of balancing emotions and teaching. "You can only inspire and fire up emotions so far," Barra said. "You must teach the fundamentals and know the right buttons to push. It's called preparation. Bear was a fanatic on preparation; he was a thorough student of the game. He did not rely on the emotion of the game because it doesn't last long."

So far in this study of Bryant's competency, we've learned he was a problem solver, a salesman, a teacher, a team builder, and was exemplary in his organizational and preparatory skills. What happened, though, when change came along? How did Bryant deal with it? Did it distract him? Was it a burden on the team? Was he flexible? Let's find out.

DEALING WITH CHANGE

For Coach Bryant, change came in two major ways — *on* the field and *off* the field. The on-the-field changes, he could pretty much control, since most were initiated by him. The off-the-field changes, though, were beyond his control, yet he was a master in dealing with each and every one of them. Let's briefly look at both.

In our Learning and Teaching segment earlier in this chapter, I mentioned a few of Bryant's innovative strategies through his career, but none was bigger than his change to the wishbone offense in 1971.

After seeing Oklahoma's wishbone gallop up and down the field for 349 rushing yards against the Tide in the 1970 Astro-Bluebonnet Bowl, Bryant began toying with the idea of making the change. But it was not until after spring practice of 1971 that he decided.

"I knew after spring training that we couldn't win with dropback passing," Bryant would later say. "We couldn't win the year before with a pro-style passer. Or the year before that. We could move up and down the field, but we couldn't get in the end zone."

The gurus of the wishbone offense were Texas head coach Darrell Royal and offensive coordinator Emory Bellard. Bryant visited Royal in 1971 to learn more about the triple option attack, then in the summer Royal and Bellard came to Tuscaloosa for a coaching clinic. Bryant and several of his assistants cornered the pair for a couple of days, and out of the pow-wow came the wishbone offense, Alabama style.

Today, with round-the-clock media coverage, radio talk shows, Internet, chat rooms, and text messaging, any team's attempt to drastically change an entire offense would be old news by suppertime. In 1971, though, the Tide's switch to the wishbone remained the best kept secret in all of college football. Even when the SEC Skywriters Tour flew into town, the crafty Bryant switched back to the old pro set for a day. Not a one of them had a clue.

Nor, for that matter, did Southern California on a hot and steamy Friday night in Los Angeles. Stunning the Trojans and head coach (and Bryant friend) John McKay, Alabama jumped out to a 17-0 lead and held on for a 17-10 victory for Bryant's 200th career win.

Bryant's move to the wishbone proved to be a spectacular decision. Over the next nine seasons, Alabama went 97-11 and won three national and eight SEC championships. "When Alabama went to the wishbone, Coach Bryant got really involved," observes Richard Williamson, an end on Alabama's 1961 national championship team. "He was like a kid with a new toy."

Changes for Bryant *off* the field were much more challenging than his on-the-field issues. First was the issue of race, about which Mickey Herskowitz commented in his book, *The Legend of Bear Bryant*. "Bear might have integrated his teams as early as his Kentucky years, and had long lamented the loss of Alabama blacks to the Big Ten and the West Coast," Herskowitz wrote. "But the pace of integration in the South was determined by politics, not by football coaches."

Although Alabama's 42-21 loss to Southern California in 1970 brought to public attention the Tide's absence of black players (and Southern Cal's *presence* of them), Bryant had already signed his first black player, Wilbur Jackson, who was on the freshman squad in 1970. Jackson would be the first of many blacks to don the Crimson and White from that point on.

Brent Musburger, long-time television sports broadcaster and currently the voice of college football for *ESPN on ABC*, said, "Coach Bryant was willing to change with the times. He led the way on integration in the SEC, among other things. A lot of veteran coaches just won't change; that's what separated him from the others."

Other issues facing Bryant – and every other coach in the country – included the Vietnam War protests, the onset of the drug culture, a change in the nation's values, long hair, and a general disrespect of authority. Let's learn first-hand how Bryant handled some of these changes.

"Coach Bryant had the ability to change when the circumstances changed," said David Mathews, University president during this time.

"When he arrived at Alabama in 1958, the college environment was not all that different from when he was a student.

"However, in the late sixties and early seventies, things changed dramatically. Long hair, war protests, not trusting anyone over thirty – it was a whole new ball game. A lot of coaches around the country couldn't deal with it, but Coach Bryant could. He didn't compromise his basic principles, but he was very skilled at relating to those new generation students. That turned out to be his most productive generation as a coach."

Former Alabama end Bill Battle, who experienced similar head coaching challenges at Tennessee in the early 1970s, adds, "It's hard to get to the top, but harder to stay at the top. That's what was so amazing about Coach Bryant. His teams won in the forties, fifties, sixties, seventies, and eighties. Think of all the changes to society over those decades, from crewcuts to long hair and beards. From 'Yes sir' and 'No sir' to questioning authority about everything.

"Coach believed that adversity is far better to deal with than prosperity. In the good times people tend to get fat-headed and lose their focus. Adversity pulls people together and gets them on the same page. You can bet that Coach had his players on the same page."

Although Bryant flowed with the various off-the-field changes, his on-the-field principles didn't waver. Darwin Holt and Murray Legg, who played for Bryant a generation apart, have similar observations.

"Coach had a winning process and developed it early on," said Holt, an early 1960s linebacker. "He changed locations from Maryland to Kentucky to Texas A&M to Alabama, but he didn't change his process of mental toughness, physical toughness, desire, and 110 percent effort. If you didn't go along, you could leave, but if you stuck it out, that process would stick with you the rest of your life."

Legg, a late 1970s defensive back, adds, "Coach could adapt to the changes in the game, but he always stuck to his principles and wouldn't sacrifice those. All the players knew that."

During the late 1960s and early 1970s, Bryant established a player committee to address the pertinent issues. Defensive back David McMakin represented the sophomore class. "As a leader, Coach Bryant was not afraid to change his mind," McMakin said. "In the 1970s the atmosphere on the campus began to change as students started all the revolutionary stuff. The campus began to look different with all the dress code issues. Coach formed a Communications Committee to discuss various issues impacting all of us. Coach would listen to us and consider the changes we'd recommend.

"Several weeks before we went out to Los Angeles to play Southern Cal in 1971, Coach said, 'I want to treat that game like a bowl trip. The guys who bust it hard and give a top effort in practice will be rewarded.' Well, the week of the game, the travel team was posted and there were several names not on the list. Right after that, we had a Communications Committee meeting to go over a list of things. At the end, Coach said, 'Anything else?'

"Well, I piped up and said, 'Weeks ago you said that this would be like a bowl trip and if players worked hard, they'd be rewarded. Why are these eight to ten guys not going?' Coach simply said, 'We're taking a team out there to win a game.'

"We left and the meeting was over. The next day a new list was posted that included those eight to ten names. Coach remembered what he'd said earlier and adjusted."

Wide receiver Wayne Wheeler, also a member of the committee, recalls other issues being brought to Bryant. "During all the uprisings of the early seventies, we wanted to be like all the other students and speak our minds," Wheeler said. "But Coach reminded us, 'You're not like the other students. You have to be better than the other students.'

"We asked for the right to grow off-season beards and let our hair grow long. I started growing a pretty good beard and let my hair get pretty long. One day I got a call from Coach to come see him at his office. He said, 'Wayne, we've got an opportunity to put you on the cover of the *Sporting News*, but you've got to get your hair cut.' I thought later, Coach let us have our way, but we really didn't have our way."

Malcolm Moran, award-winning sports journalist for *The New York Times* and *USA Today*, puts into perspective Bryant's leadership. "Coach Bryant's ability to adapt made him a great leader," said Moran, now the Knight Chair in Sports Journalism at Penn State. "His teams succeeded with the passing of Joe Namath and Ken Stabler, but the Tide also won with the precision of the triple option.

"His authoritative approach endured even as attitudes among college students – including athletes – changed dramatically in the 1960s and early 1970s. His support of the acceptance of African-American athletes was considered an important part of the integration of Alabama football. And although the treatment of his Texas A&M players – the Junction Boys – was glorified in many corners, he eventually felt that he had been too harsh."

BALANCE

Balance between professional life and personal life may have been Coach Bryant's greatest weakness, which is probably the same with all the great leaders. We get consumed, we get swept away, and we get focused on the tasks at hand, while our families sit at home, wondering when we'll walk through the door.

Even Bryant hinted at this. "I've had a full life in one respect, but I've had a one-track deal in another respect," he once said. "My life has been so tied up with football it has flown by. I wish it wasn't that way, but it has gone by mighty fast. Practice, recruiting and games; there hasn't been anything except football."

Lack of balance is especially true in sports, when it's all about winning and the "if you don't win, you're gone" mentality. So, in many cases, you work out of a fear of failure.

Legendary UCLA basketball coach John Wooden said the two most important words in the English language were "love" and "balance." Balance not only on your feet, on the court, or on the field, but balance in your life – taking care of your health, your spiritual life, and your relationship with your family.

There's no question that Coach Bryant would probably say he was not the most balanced person in the world. But all great leaders fight this every day.

However, after listening to two of Bryant's grandchildren, Marc Tyson and his sister Mary Harmon Tyson Moman, reminisce about life with their grandfather, I came to the realization that Bryant had more balance in his life than you may think.

Tyson, Bryant's only grandson of five grandchildren, is president of Ready Mix USA, one of several companies owned by Bryant's son, Paul, Jr. "We called him 'Papa' and our grandmother was 'Gran,'" said Tyson, son of Bryant's daughter, Mae Martin Tyson. "He loved his family and his players were part of that family. He enjoyed spending time with all of us.

"Gran was a real mother to the players. Many of them had never been on an airplane before and she'd get them calmed down. And, she would help them write letters to their families back home.

"On game days, Papa would be on the first bus and Gran on the second," continued Tyson, who was a student at Alabama when Bryant died. "The players all wanted to be on her bus because she would talk to them and Papa was stone cold silent. Gran would come to meals at the dorm and say to the players, 'Come and sit with us.' They didn't want to do that because Papa scared them."

Tyson's many treasured moments with his grandfather are ingrained in his mind to this day. "Some of my most vivid memories," Tyson said, "are packing up presents on Christmas day and going to Papa's and Gran's house in Tuscaloosa, going bream fishing with him using cane poles and crickets, and quail hunting at Jimmy Hinton's place at Sedgefield Plantation. Papa couldn't wait to get out there.

"Papa was also a big baseball fan and took me to see the Yankees, Red Sox, and Reds play one year. We had a great time. I just wish more people could have seen this side of him.

"Papa was really a funny guy. I was a pretty good high school football player, and one Friday night I had had a good game and he was one proud grandfather. He was all over town bragging about me. He just went on and on. One fellow asked him, 'Is the boy good enough to play at Alabama?' Papa answered, 'He ain't *that* good.'"

Marc's older sister, Mary Harmon Tyson Moman, shares similar stories of Bryant's love for all his grandchildren. "I was the oldest grandchild, so my first memory of him was sitting on the floor and playing Barbie dolls with me," Moman said. "He'd take me to Shoney's to get a hamburger and we'd use that carhop service they had because he'd get mobbed if we went inside to eat. As a child, I'd get trampled by people trying to get his autograph. I did theater as a child and he'd come to see my plays.

"My grandmother was a lady at all levels. The football players viewed her as a mother to the whole squad. They'd come to her with all their problems. I remember she'd always carry mints or gum in her purse to hand out.

"Papa was very much into children and how much they counted and how important they were. He'd stop and sign autographs until every youngster was taken care of.

"Whenever I had a little problem, he'd tell me, 'Suck up your guts.' In other words, just go on; it won't have that big of an impact on your life.

"He was very big on the present moment. I can still hear him saying, 'You need to do something today.' That meant get busy and don't waste time, because you can't get it back. Something he told me that has impacted me greatly is, 'With everyone you encounter each day, imagine that they won't live past midnight.'

"Papa also told us to 'Believe in yourself and then go about your dream with dedication and pride. Don't quit and keep going if you believe in it.'"

Pat Trammell, Jr., son of the famed quarterback from the 1961 national championship team, recalls Bryant making him feel such a part of his family. "Coach Bryant treated me like a grandson," said Trammell, whose father died of cancer on December 10, 1968, a day that Bryant would later call "the saddest day of my life."

"I was just a little kid but he made me feel so important. Every year before the season started, I'd get a package with a sideline pass and all sorts of football info. Every Christmas and on my birthday I'd get a gift from Coach. There are thousands of stories like that of Coach serving people without any fanfare. That's real leadership to me – leadership done with a serving heart.

"After Keith Jackson retired at ABC, the network did an in-depth feature on his broadcasting career. Keith was asked about the highlight of his career. He said, 'I was sitting in Coach Bryant's office one day when the phone rang. The news was not good. Coach was informed that Pat Trammell's cancer had returned. I saw Bryant break down and weep in front of me. That moment will live with me forever.'"

As you can see, Bryant did have some balance after all, juggling on-the-field duties with fishing trips, dove hunting, baseball excursions, hamburgers at Shoney's, and dates with Barbie dolls. In the final chapter, we'll discuss some more of Bryant's serving heart traits.

CHARISMA

Okay, here we go. I looked up "charisma" in the dictionary and lo and behold, I saw a picture of Bear Bryant. Well, in my dictionary, at least.

Of all the memories I heard from the more than 200 people interviewed for this book, references to Bryant's charisma wins the prize, especially all those "when he walked into the room" comments. Let's listen in on their remembrances.

"I went to the famous 1979 Sugar Bowl with Penn State playing Alabama for the national title," said Ernie Accorsi, former Penn State sports information director. "The night before the game, there was a reception at the old Roosevelt Hotel in the second floor ballroom. I will never forget when Bear Bryant entered the room. He filled it up with his presence and charisma. He towered over Joe Paterno, who must've felt he was in the presence of a superior coach."

Leon Ashford, a student trainer in the late 1960s, said, "Coach could walk in a room and command attention and respect, almost like the President of the United States. Yet he never became arrogant or haughty. He didn't like all the public attention, yet he was always serene and in charge."

Jimmy Bank, son of long-time Alabama radio network producer Bert Bank, said, "It was fascinating to go on the road with the Alabama team. Coach Bryant would walk through the hotel lobby packed with fans and you could see people stepping aside like a parting of the waters.

"One year I traveled to Seattle for the Alabama-Washington game. I went out to the stadium early and went to the big luxury suite where all the big Washington boosters were dining. Suddenly the Alabama team appeared on the field down below and you could hear the buzz among the boosters – 'Where is he? Oh, there he is! See him standing over there. He's the one with the hat on.'"

Paul Boschung, a defensive tackle in 1967-69, said, "Coach was an imposing figure and awe-inspiring, especially to a freshman. There was no one bigger. You knew you were in the presence of greatness."

I will say that of all the "when he walked into the room" comments I heard, Byron Braggs' was the most unique. "Coach would meet with us every day," said Braggs, a four-year letterman in 1977-80. "He'd turn the corner and come into that auditorium and you could hear a cockroach die on cotton. Then he'd talk to us, and not about football. He'd teach a life lesson each day from a little booklet called 'Bits 'n Pieces.' His message was, 'Life is like football – you've got to work hard to get anything.'"

Sylvester Croom, whose father Sylvester, Sr. served as Alabama team chaplain for many years, said, "The first time I met Coach Bryant as an 18-year old kid, I was awed at how big he was. He was 6'-4" tall, well-built, and ruggedly handsome. His walk and his gait were just like John Wayne. He carried himself in a unique manner. He dressed well and looked good. The man had style. When Coach walked in, he took over the room. Men feared him and women loved him. He had it all and would be a cover guy today."

"Bear Bryant had charisma," said former Georgia Tech and Alabama head coach Bill Curry, who was 1-2 against Bryant while with the Yellow Jackets. "He could walk into a room or on a field and it changed. It was a boldness that he had. When he walked onto a field, people started palpitating."

Former Georgia head coach Vince Dooley remarked, "Coach was an impressive man with that tall and erect stature. He looked like a great military general. He'd walk into a room and all eyes would open up. He commanded an audience."

Dennis Goehring, a guard and graduate assistant for Bryant at Texas A&M, said, "There was a charisma about the man that made everybody stand up and pay attention. He commanded that kind of respect and did it better than anyone I've ever been around."

Noted author Winston Groom was a student at Alabama from 1961-65 and watched two of Bryant's national championship teams in action. "I saw Coach Bryant as a stern taskmaster with a formidable personality," Groom said. "Everywhere he went, he commanded enormous respect."

Tide All-American linebacker Mike Hall said, "Coach Bryant had an aura about him. He'd walk into a room with noisy conversation going on and the place would go dead silent. Someone once said that you could hear your own heart beating. Mal Moore quipped, 'I could hear the heartbeat of the guy next to me.' Coach had an intimidating presence and he'd use it to reach his goals."

Mickey Herskowitz, author of *The Legend of Bear Bryant,* one of the three definitive biographies on Bryant, remembers that "Coach Bryant had a leadership presence that was nothing short of Douglas MacArthur. When he got to Texas A&M, he was just 39 and looked like a movie star and a Mount Rushmore figure. He had the John Wayne look – a smooth unwrinkled face and towering physical presence. He was about 6'-4" and 220 and in great shape.

"All the movies and image makers of Bryant portray him as a savage tyrant. But, as one old A&M player said to me, 'If he was so evil to us, why do we love him so much?'"

A favorite of Tide fans is Colin "Big C" MacGuire, a student manager from 1977-80. While working for Bryant, MacGuire noticed the coach's charisma in the form of respect. "When Coach wanted you to do something, you did it because you didn't want to let him down. We all respected him so much."

Former Tennessee head coach Johnny Majors had only one victory in six tries against Bryant. Listening to him reminisce makes one wonder if he, too, wasn't intimidated by the Tide's head man. "Coach Bryant had a real advantage with his size," Majors said. "He was big physically, which was impressive, plus he had good looks. He was tall, broad-shouldered, and square-jawed. He had a raw-boned look and a look of strength on his face. He was a handsome man and his slow gaited walk helped create an aura about him."

For Wes Neighbors, being around Bryant was a once-in-a-lifetime honor. "When Coach Bryant walked in a room," he said, "we'd stop what we were doing. It was like the air was sucked right out of the room. His very presence commanded respect. I've never been around a person like that before or since."

One of Alabama's most revered all-time players is Major Ogilvie, a running back from 1977-80. Ogilvie, team captain in 1980, said, "Coach had a very powerful personality and was a special person in our lives. He impacted everyone he met. Coach could walk in a room and all the attention turned toward him. The man had so many intangible qualities. It's impossible to capture him in a sentence, a paragraph, or a page. Entire books have been devoted to him and still we want more."

Just the nickname "Bear" brought charisma to Bryant, says Billy Pickard, Bryant's student trainer at Texas A&M. "If you ever heard someone tell you, 'Bear Bryant and me are tight,' they weren't," Pickard said. "If someone said, 'Coach Bryant and I were this, that, or the other, they were. People close to him never referred to him as 'Bear.' It was always 'Coach.'"

As we've heard, Bryant's presence at Bryant Hall, the athletic dorm, had its good and bad moments. As Keith Pugh recalls, "We could be eating dinner – 85 or 90 guys with dishes clanging – and when Coach Bryant walked in, everyone got quiet. Of course, it helps to be a leader when you're 6'-4" and 240 pounds. He was so intimidating and just his presence commanded respect."

"Coach Bryant was born to lead," said Jack Rutledge. "All you had to do was be in his presence and you'd understand that statement. Whenever he'd enter a room, call a meeting, attend a pep rally, or call a players' powwow, he had the total attention of everyone. You couldn't hear a sound. That was part of his leadership gift."

Barry Smith, a late 1970s snapper, added, "Coach Bryant could walk in a room and the hair would stand up on your head. You'd feel a chill come over you. There'd be a murmur in the room and then a buzz. The man had a presence that was exciting to be around."

Defensive end Russ Wood played on Bryant's last four teams, including the games in which Bryant tied (#314) and surpassed (#315) Amos Alonzo Stagg's all-time winning record. As well, Wood's ferocious defensive play helped secure Bryant's final victory in the 1982 Liberty Bowl. Wood shares some Bryant charisma stories from each game.

"At the 314 game at Penn State, their fans were lined up three deep trying to see Coach Bryant," Wood said. "We heard them yelling, 'Where's your coach? Where's Bear?' We had never been to State College before, and most of them had never seen him in person.

"After Coach set the record against Auburn in the 315 game, President Reagan called him in the locker room. Coach called him the

'Gipper' and made the president stutter. There's Ronald Reagan, an established actor and communicator, and Coach Bryant has him stuttering on the phone. That's the kind of charisma he had.

"At the Liberty Bowl luncheon in 1982, there were 2,000 people in attendance at the Civic Center. Coach Eddie Robinson was being honored that day. The players were sitting at tables with the fans. Obviously there was a lot of noise with dishes clanging and people talking and laughing. Suddenly the whole place went stone cold quiet. I said, 'Coach Bryant just came in.' One of the fans asked, 'How did you know?' I replied, 'We've seen it before.'"

HISTORY

Great leaders understand the background of any organization. You must know your company's history and the culture that drives it.

You can't just come into any organization because you're the new leader on the block and just obliterate all the history of that organization. If you do, you're making a grave mistake.

Coach Bryant sure believed in his organization, not only in the Alabama football program, but in the University of Alabama. After all, the University was special to him. As a student in the 1930s, he had smelled the Quad's freshly cut grass on his way to classes. He had played on the turf of 12,000-seat Denny Stadium and witnessed the stadium's first expansion in the mid-1930s. He had tasted a national championship in 1934, and had even met his wife-to-be, Mary Harmon Black, on campus.

So when Bryant returned as head coach in 1958 and walked out on the field for spring practice, no one was surprised when he said, "There's not a spot of ground out there that doesn't have a little of my blood on it."

With his passion for the school is undeniable, Bryant proceeded to build his football program on the tradition established years earlier by Xen Scott, Wallace Wade, Frank Thomas, and Harold "Red" Drew. Like a construction company erecting a skyscraper, Bryant built Alabama football toward the sky, one floor at a time.

In his 25 years as Alabama's head coach, his teams won 14 SEC and six national championships and he became, by the time he retired, the winningest college football coach of all time. "I still get chills when they play those old fight songs and the Alabama alma mater," Bryant would say. "If that's corny, then I'm corny."

Bryant, though, was emphatic that tradition could only get you so far, often citing a balance between it and the game itself. "You don't win on tradition; you win on blocking and tackling on the field," he said. "But I do think tradition is important in that it gives the players and coaches something to live up to."

ACCEPT AUTHORITY

No matter how high on the food chain Coach Bryant was, he still had authority over him, namely the school's president and board of trustees. There is someone in authority over everybody in leadership, and if you lose sight of that, you're headed for a fall.

In his 25 seasons at Alabama, Bryant worked for three sitting presidents (excluding interims) – Frank Rose (1957-69), David Mathews (1969-1980), and Joab Thomas (1981-82).

Rose came to Alabama in 1957, just in time to hear the moans and groans of the Crimson Tide football faithful, who were suffering through the J.B. "Ears" Whitworth era. By mid-October of 1957, Whitworth received word that his services as head football coach had been appreciated, but no longer needed.

Whitworth's three-year record of 4-24-2 set the stage for Bryant's hiring, which officially took place on December 3, 1957. At a press conference in Houston, Texas, Bryant announced he was heading back to Alabama because, as he affectionately said, "Mama called." Rose boasted that Alabama had just hired "the greatest football coach in America." Never in his life was he more accurate.

The youthful David Mathews succeeded Rose as president in 1969. To this day, Mathews cherishes his memories of the University and considered it pure joy to work alongside Bryant.

"I was 33 years old when I arrived as the president of the University," Mathews said. "Coach Bryant was deep into his career and one of the most famous people in the country. Due to our age difference, he could have recoiled at the indignity, but he didn't. He had a fierce sense of loyalty to the University and he accepted me at once.

"As a leader, he was impressive with the manner in which he dealt with defeat. He believed that winning begins with losing. When I first got to Alabama, he had had back-to-back 6-5 seasons, which is like going 0-11 at Alabama. I started getting calls to fire him, that he's past his prime, that if you don't fire him we'll get *you* fired.

"Then his successes started to come in the seventies and that prevented a nosedive. There was a consistency with him as he dealt with his critics. He always said, 'If the Coach doesn't win, the alumni ought to fire him. I'm a member of the alumni, so I'll lead the charge.'

"Coach Bryant may have been the last of the coaches who put education above winning and character above championships. Paul Bryant's lasting contribution is not in the games he won, but in the lives he touched. He was one of the best teachers I ever saw."

Joab Thomas, who followed Mathews in 1981, shares similar thoughts about Bryant and his love for the University. "Many people thought Coach Bryant was an independent entity unto himself and his football program," Thomas said. "That was not the case. He was totally dedicated to supporting the University and all that we were doing. He was easy to work with and made our relationship a pleasant and rewarding experience."

Of my many interviews for this book, one of the most detailed and revealing came from C.M. Newton, whom Coach Bryant hired as the Tide's head basketball coach in 1968. I'll leave you with his thoughts on what made Bryant a competent and successful leader.

BRYANT'S KEY QUALITIES AS A LEADER

1. His great work ethic; he would outwork anybody.
2. He delegated well, but also maintained control. This is a delicate point, but everyone knew who the boss was.
3. He was a great listener.
4. He was eager to learn and as a result was receptive to different ways of doing things.
5. He was willing to change with the times and not just the issue of recruiting black athletes.
6. He had great self-confidence.
7. He was a top salesman, but did it in a low-key way.
8. He was not aloof as some people thought, but was really a shy person. He enjoyed the attention he received, but didn't seek it.
9. He was willing to make tough decisions, particularly related to areas of discipline.
10. He genuinely cared about his players and he showed it.
11. He was very intelligent. He'd give you that old Arkansas plowboy stuff with all the mumbling, but he was on the cutting edge of everything, like rules, recruiting, etc.
12. He enjoyed his role as a mentor and teacher.

"I firmly believe Coach Bryant could've been governor or president," Newton observed. "He would have been successful at whatever he chose. His leadership ability would have allowed him to do anything he wanted to pursue. He just chose football as his career path."

Chapter Six

BOLDNESS

"I'm through tiptoeing around, and I'm through pussyfooting around. I'm going back to being Paul Bryant, and anybody who doesn't like the way Paul Bryant does things can get the heck out of here."
—PAUL W. "BEAR" BRYANT

At the end of the day, leaders must be bold and make decisions. In the White House, George W. Bush used to say, "I'm the decider, and I decide what to do."

Well, wherever Coach Bryant roamed the sidelines, from College Park to Lexington to College Station to Tuscaloosa, he was unequivocally the decision-maker. He believed so much in his program and his mission that he was never fearful to make the final decision and live with the consequences.

Bryant left Maryland after only one season because the school president fired one of his assistants and reinstated a player he had dismissed from the team. At Kentucky, despite his unparalleled success on the gridiron, Bryant played second fiddle to basketball legend Adolph Rupp, although their personal relationship was harmonious. When sanctions came down penalizing the Kentucky basketball program in 1952-53, Bryant's football program, although having done no wrong, was the victim of newly-established recruiting limitations.

Bryant felt as though the administration had reneged on its commitment to him and Kentucky football.

Even before Bryant accepted the Alabama jobs of head coach and athletic director, he made sure that his old coach, Hank Crisp, who had been serving as athletic director, was taken care of in some capacity. Bryant was adamant that if "Coach Hank" had not been accommodated, he would have never made the move to Tuscaloosa. Bryant was a man of principle, a strong believer in a man's word being his bond.

DECISIVENESS

The phrase "The buck stops here," popularized by President Harry Truman, was quite appropriate for Coach Bryant. "The buck stops here" just means that the authority figure – in this case Bryant – has to make the decisions and accept the ultimate responsibility for those decisions.

With Bryant, there was never any hesitation to make the call. It takes courage to do that in difficult issues and decisions. Who's going to be the starter? Who are we offering a scholarship to? In pro sports, it's who's going to be traded? Who's going to get cut?

From those who were around Bryant, let's see how his boldness and decisiveness came into play. We'll start by hearing from two pioneers in Alabama athletics history – Wendell Hudson, the first black to sign an athletic (basketball) scholarship at Alabama, and Walter Lewis, Alabama's first black starting quarterback.

"Coach Bryant was not afraid to lead, which means he would step out and do what he thought was right," said Hudson, who entered Alabama in the fall of 1969. "He was willing to make decisions and then have a plan in place to back them up. Coach understood that when you make a decision, it is yours and you have to stand up, take responsibility and live with the consequences."

Lewis, a four-year football letterman from 1980-83, aptly describes Bryant's decision making prowess. "The Kenny Rogers song 'The Gambler' describes Coach Bryant as a leader – 'You gotta know when to hold 'em, know when to fold 'em, and when to walk away,'" Lewis said. "In other words, as a leader you've got to make decisions and not look back.

"All great leaders are willing to stand in the gap for those underneath them. I was the first black quarterback at Alabama in 1980 and I'm sure Coach took the heat on that. I'm sure a lot of people wanted him to do something different. He protected me and did what he thought was best for the team."

Ozzie Newsome, Tide All-American receiver from 1974-77, makes hard decisions every day as general manager of the NFL's Baltimore Ravens. He credits Bryant with teaching him how. "Coach Bryant could make the tough decision," Newsome said. "He believed that if you trust your instincts, you'll make the right decision. He didn't just make the decision; he was great on following through. He would see it all the way to the finish.

"In my role as an NFL general manager, several of Coach Bryant's leadership principles have been valuable to me. First, let the information make the decision. If you get the right information, it'll lead to the right decision. Second, work intelligently and don't waste time putting in long hours that aren't productive. Third, if you make a bad decision, go back through the process and figure out where things went wrong. And fourth, never compromise the team. Set your standards and don't operate on exceptions, otherwise all you'll do is deal with those exceptions."

Tubby Raymond, longtime football coach at the University of Delaware, had the opportunity to serve on Bryant's staff at an All-Star game in Lubbock, Texas. Raymond sensed something very special while working alongside Bryant. "Coach had such a stance; you thought he could do anything," Raymond said. "He would think about a situation and then make his decision quickly. You felt he was tapped right in and had information the rest of us didn't have."

During Bryant's 25-year tenure at Alabama, no one wore more hats than Gary White, whose 39-year service to Alabama athletics included three years as head student manager and later as dorm director, academic counselor, compliance officer, and associate athletic director. White dealt with Bryant and the myriad of decisions that had to be made on a daily basis.

"Coach Bryant was great at decision-making," White said. "One night a kid at the dorm was out all night and Coach found out about it. He got all the information first before dealing with it. He asked me for my opinion and if I thought his solution would solve the problem. I told him yes and he went ahead with the decision. That's the way he went about things. Any decisions of his were not made in haste and not without first consulting his staff."

Bryant's off-the-field decisions may not have been made in haste, but the same couldn't be said for his – or any coach's – on-field decisions. Keith Jackson, the most definitive voice in college football broadcasting history, recalls a particular sideline decision of Bryant's that proved, as usual, a good one. "Bear was a good sideline coach and could make quick decisions," Jackson said. "I did the Alabama-Tennessee game one year in Knoxville. By the end of the first quarter, it was raining pretty good. Bear was discussing the offense with his coordinator, Mal Moore, and trying to get something going.

"Bear says to Mal, 'See that #11 over there? Put him in.' I don't think Bear even knew his name, but the kid runs the play, all the blocks are perfect, and no one lays a hand on him as he goes 37 yards for a game-winning touchdown. More often than not, those sideline decisions turned out just right."

CONFIDENCE

It takes courage to confront difficult issues and make difficult decisions. So, from where does this courage come? It comes from having confidence in what you're doing. And from where does this confidence come? It comes from experience, from paying your dues, from "been there, done that."

When Bryant was hired at Alabama, he wasn't thrown into a leadership role for the first time. The man had been around the block many, many times. He had paid his dues growing up in Moro Bottom and Fordyce, Arkansas, where he learned the value of hard work; at Alabama, where he grew into a man; in his assistant coaching stops at Alabama and Vanderbilt, where he enhanced his football know-how; in the Navy in World War II, where he learned sacrifice; and finally in his head coaching stops at Maryland, Kentucky, Texas A&M, and Alabama.

As a leader, you must be willing to pay your dues down in the trenches and learn your business from the ground up. Without that experience, you're incomplete as a leader.

As an athletic student trainer from 1966-70, Leon Ashford quickly noticed Bryant's confidence. "When I was 18 years old, I wasn't observing Coach Bryant as a leader, but today at 62, I am," Ashford said. "He was supremely and intensely self-confident. He believed in his way or the highway. There was nothing contrived about Coach as a leader; he had it. He was totally confident in his approach."

Birmingham native Bobby Bowden, recently retired head coach at Florida State, never faced Bryant on the field, but learned many lessons from him nevertheless. "He was an intimidating man," Bowden said.

"As a young coach, I hung around Tuscaloosa with his assistants. They were scared to death of him, and of course I was, too. I thought, 'Is he as tough as he seems?' I've never seen someone so confident in what he was doing."

Mike McKenzie, sports editor of *The Tuscaloosa News* in the mid-1970s, quickly found out what a confident and commanding person Bryant was. "As a leader, the man had such command and self-confidence," McKenzie said. "In December of 1974, Alabama was getting ready to play Notre Dame in the Orange Bowl. Both teams were ranked, so it was a big game. This was my first year in Tuscaloosa, so I wanted to get off to a good start.

"I set up an appointment with Coach Bryant and met him in his office. My first question was, 'Well, Coach, what's Santa Claus going to bring you this year?' He growled back, 'Well, I *am* Santa Claus.'

"That was the interview. I couldn't get a second question ready. However, that summed up the man as a leader. He was in command of his world and exuded self-confidence. He walked the talk. He didn't have to say much, but when he spoke you heard him."

As former sports editor of *The Huntsville Times*, John Pruett makes an interesting observation of Bryant's confidence. "There was a real dichotomy to Coach Bryant," Pruett said. "He was driven to be the best, yet he was afraid to fail and go back to plowing.

"On the other hand, he would walk into a room and display great self-confidence and declare, 'I ain't nothing but a winner' when asked what he wanted to be remembered for."

Alvin Samples, an Alabama All-American guard in 1969, adds, "As a leader, Coach Bryant walked the walk and didn't just talk the talk. He was well established in his profession and had great confidence as a leader. His philosophy was built around hard work, dedication and devotion to the task. Set goals and work hard to get them."

Gary Rutledge, quarterback on the Tide's 1973 national championship squad, reminds us that not only did Bryant *have* confidence, but he *taught* it as well. "Coach Bryant's favorite phrase with his quarterbacks was 'poise and confidence,'" said Rutledge, whose younger brother Jeff also won a national championship with Alabama in 1978. "During his famous walks with his quarterbacks before the games, he'd always remind us that we couldn't lose our poise. He would say, 'When things are not going well, be a leader. You can't let your teammates see you in the huddle with fear in your eyes.' He wanted us to be bold and have confidence."

On many occasions, Bryant's boldness shone brightly just by his actions. Some may have been behind closed doors in his office, while some may have been on the field of play. No matter where or when, the memories still resonate.

"I played all three major sports at Kentucky, which included four years for Adolph Rupp and three for Coach Bryant," said Wah Wah Jones, who from 1947-49 made All-SEC in all three sports, All-American in two, and played on three NCAA basketball title teams for Rupp. "Coach Bryant was firm in what he wanted done. I had an opportunity to try out for the old Boston Braves and asked his advice. He stared at me and in his own bold way, said, 'Are you going to play football or baseball?' I piped up and said, 'Football, sir.' That was it for the baseball tryout. You did what he wanted you to do because you wanted to please him.

"Bryant was a big man at 6'-4" and strong and tough. I played end at Kentucky and went both ways. He'd get down on the line with you and knock you down and then you'd hear him say, 'Now, that's the way to do it!'"

Dennis Goehring, a player and graduate assistant coach for Bryant at Texas A&M, recalls negotiating a "deal" between him and the coach. "I came to A&M without a scholarship and hardly played as a freshman," Goehring said. "After that season, I went up to Coach Bryant's office and asked if I could get a scholarship.

"He said, 'No.' I said, 'Why not?' He said, 'Because you're not a football player.' Then I said, 'Coach, I'll make a deal with you.' He said, 'What kind of deal?' I said, 'If I make the team, you'll give me a scholarship.'

"Coach replied, 'OK, I'll make that deal with you.' By mid-season of my sophomore year I was a starter and played two-way football the rest of my career. I wasn't going to let him intimidate me. Bryant appreciated people who stood up to him and took exception to what he was saying. If you did that, you'd gain his respect. He didn't want you to give into him, but to buck him a little bit. I guess he liked folks being bold with him sometimes."

Jimmy Fuller, a member of the 1964 and 1965 Alabama national championship teams, said, "Coach Bryant grew up tough and hard and was tough on his players. He was trying to make us all that we could be. As a result I did everything I could to give him what he expected.

"I was having one of those perfect days at practice as I headed into my sophomore year. Everything was coming together perfectly with my blocking and tackling. Then we heard the chain noise and Coach was down off the tower.

"He came over to me and said, 'How do you think you're doing?' I said, 'I'm really having a good day, Coach.' Then he said, 'If you think you are good enough to play on my football team, you are badly mistaken.' The man always kept you on edge, but I respect him and love him to this day."

Okay, let's take a quick detour here. Jimmy Fuller just mentioned Bryant's famous (or infamous) tower on which he would perch, giving him a bird's eye view of all going on down below. Talk about boldness!

In Bryant's own brilliant way, the 33-step tower not only gave him a visual advantage, but a psychological one as well.

"I think the tower was a symbol of 'I'm up here and you're down there and you'd better not make a mistake because I'm going to see it,'" said the late *Birmingham News* sportswriter Jimmy Bryan, in an ESPN Sports Century Classic interview.

Gene Stallings, an assistant coach at Alabama from 1958-64 and head coach from 1990-96, added, "You hated to have a drill right under the tower. I'd think of him picking up that bullhorn and saying, 'Coach Stallings, that's one of the worst drills I've ever seen.'"

Bill Curry, Stallings' predecessor at Alabama, said, "Coach Bryant would be up in that practice tower and he might spot a pro scout or a university official – it could be anyone – and you'd hear his voice through his bullhorn. He'd be ordering you up to his tower. My goodness, it was as if you were ascending to the heavens."

You may remember Mickey Herskowitz's comment in the first chapter about Bryant seemingly having a "third eye." In other words, he didn't miss a thing, and the tower only enhanced his perspective.

Danny Ford, a player in the late 1960s and assistant coach in the early 1970s, recalls Bryant's "third eye" trait. "We'd have two scrimmages going on at the same time and Coach would be up in his tower watching all of it. He wouldn't miss a thing. You felt his eyes were on you all the time. After each play, coaches and players alike would look up at that tower to make sure he wasn't coming down."

Gary Rutledge was one of many players who kept a close watch on Bryant's tower. "If Coach lost his temper, you didn't want to be on the receiving end," said Rutledge, who's best known for his 80-yard touchdown bomb to Wayne Wheeler on the first play of the 1973 Alabama-Tennessee game. "The best thing to do was always hustle. You didn't want to see him leave that tower during practice. The only time he came down was if he was mad and he was going to chew on someone. If he stayed in the tower, things were going well."

As intimidating as the tower was, it was the rattle of the tower's chain that commanded everyone's attention. "We'd rather hear the sound of a shotgun going off at night than hear the sound of that chain rattling when Coach Bryant came charging out of the tower onto the practice field upset over something," said Paul Boschung, a late 1960s lineman.

This tower of power proved to be quite a symbol for Bryant's boldness and authority. Today, the tower sits overlooking the University of Alabama practice fields, fittingly unused and reserved only for a special memory.

Let's keep looking at some other examples of Bryant's boldness.

Tide All-American quarterback Joe Namath, who would go on to NFL fame with the New York Jets, received a strong dose of Bryant's boldness following his sophomore season in 1962. "As a sophomore I won a letter," Namath said. "But even so, you had to go through A-Club initiation to become a member. I wanted no part of that. If you had earned the letter, why not wear it? I didn't believe I had to go through all that initiation abuse. I didn't think it was right.

"Well, at that point I got a call to report to Coach Bryant's office. That was not good news and I tried to figure out where I had messed up.

"Coach said to me, 'Come on, I want to take a ride.' We got in his car and took off. He was quiet, very quiet, until he was ready to talk. I just sat and waited. It was very uncomfortable in that car.

"Then he said, 'Joe, I understand you won't go through the A-Club initiation.' 'That's right,' I said. Coach replied, 'Well, it's a tradition and those kinds of things are important here at Alabama. The rest of the players are going through it.'

"Then I said, 'I still don't think it's right.' Coach came back at me, 'If you don't get initiated you can't be elected captain.' I had an answer for that: 'That's the last thing on my mind. It's not a goal for me. All I care about is winning.'

"I could see he was getting really frustrated with me. His voice got louder and he barked out, 'Well, I want you to!'

"My last statement was, 'Yes, sir, I'll go through it.'"

Much has been said through the years about the 1965 Tennessee game in Legion Field when on fourth down, quarterback Kenny Stabler, thinking it was third down, threw a pass out of bounds, ending the game. Bryant didn't take the tie too well, nor did Alabama's locker room door, which he knocked off the hinges with his shoulder. If anyone is to blame for not having the door unlocked, it's probably Jim Bowman.

"For some reason that I can't explain today, another manager put the locker room key around my neck at halftime," said Bowman, a freshman student manager at the time. "After every game, the freshman managers had to stay on the field and watch the equipment. So I was out there doing my job when (trainer) Sang Lyda runs up and yells, 'Jim, you have the key to our dressing room!'

"When I got there, the door was lying on the floor, hinges torn from the wall. I later found out that when Coach Bryant got to the locked door, he instructed Chief Smelley, his state trooper, to 'shoot the lock off.' Chief Smelley said he couldn't do that as the ricochet might kill someone. So Coach told him to get out of the way.

"Needless to say, I was very embarrassed and assumed my short career at Alabama had ended. But, I managed to hold on and was a manager for the next four years. Although Coach was mad that day, he later apologized to the team and took all the blame for the tie. He told the players that they still had a shot at the national title, and sure enough, we won it."

Pat Raines experienced the lows of the 1969 (6-5-0) and 1970 (6-5-1) seasons and the highs of Bryant's first two wishbone teams in 1971-72. In an office visit to Bryant one day, Raines saw first-hand how direct Bryant could be. "One time I disagreed with him and wanted to have a meeting," Raines said. "I went to his office and he locked the door behind us. I was scared to death and thought I may never get out again.

"I told him, 'Coach, I don't like it here. Yes, I came to play football, but I want to have a good time and do some regular college stuff.' He stared at me and then said, 'Don't like it, huh? Then leave. Have a good time? Not when your record is six-and-five.' That day, I finally saw the light about the mission of Alabama football."

Mike Raines, Pat's brother, played defensive tackle for the Tide from 1970-73. He shares an eerily similar story about a visit to Bryant's office. "There was no question who the leader of our team was," Mike said. "Coach Bryant emphasized four things in this order: God, family, education, and then football. Sometimes I wondered about the order.

"Coach had some simple, bold rules, and we all knew them: Miss curfew and you were gone. Bad grades, and you were suspended until your grades improved; if they didn't, you were gone. Bad example and character off the field, and you were gone. Work as hard as him and his assistants, and you'd get a chance to play. Be on time, or meet him in his office. And believe me, you didn't want to go there.

"He had a couch in his office that you didn't want to sit in because he had the legs shortened so when you looked up at him he seemed to be ten feet tall as he smoked his Chesterfield kings. As you went in, he would lock the door behind you. Talk about scary; there was no way out.

"And then he would say what he had on his mind; basically something like this, 'So I understand you don't like the way things are run around here.' Sometimes you would respond and sometimes you wouldn't, but his comment was always the same: 'If you don't like it, leave.'"

Wes Neighbors, a redshirted freshman on Bryant's last team in 1982, once witnessed first-hand Bryant's boldness on the practice field. "At 69 years of age, Coach was still a powerful man," said Wes, who along with uncle Sid, father Billy, and younger brother Keith all wore the Crimson and White. "One day at practice, he got upset with a player's effort. This was a guy in full uniform and Coach just picked him up and his feet were off the ground, just dangling there. Coach was shaking him back and forth.

"Then Coach put the kid through a tackling drill and then kicked him off the team. The next year that guy bounced back and had a great year. He'd been heading down the wrong path and I think Coach saved him from destruction. The man had a way with people."

Tom McEwen, sports editor of *The Tampa Tribune* for 33 years, and Edwin Pope, long-time sports columnist in Atlanta and Miami, share humorous stories of Bryant's boldness.

"Coach Bryant was always in complete control," McKewen said. "One year he brought one of his Kentucky teams to play Florida at Phillips Field in Tampa. The place was packed and fans were edged right down to the sidelines. They pushed so hard that they poured all over the Kentucky players. Bear saw this and barked out, 'If you don't get back in the stands, I'm going to leave right now!' They all backed up on signal. It was the darndest thing I had ever seen."

Pope recalls Bryant's confidence, saying, "Coach had a quiet belief in himself which gives you a unique power. I've hardly seen that replicated. You have it or you don't have it and Bryant had it. He carried himself like a military general, giving you the feeling he was always in charge. But he did this in a very quiet way and never raised his voice. He didn't have to. You couldn't dislike Bryant. He had a very quiet winning way about him.

"I once wrote in a column that Bryant was ruthless. His wife objected and let me know. Funny, but I think Bear kind of liked it and took pride in it."

Chapter Seven

SERVING HEART

"Coach Bryant said to me, 'Marty, give
of yourself so others can grow.'"
—MARTY LYONS
Alabama defensive tackle, 1975-78

"Coach Bryant was known as a disciplinarian and a taskmaster,
but he was caring. I knew he cared for me and that's why I love him."
—JOHN DAVID CROW
Texas A&M running back, 1954-57, Heisman Trophy Winner, 1957

There are many six-sided leaders out there, and they're doing a good job and are worthy of our support and admiration. However, to be a leader for the ages, a leader they'll write books about, a leader who'll go down in the history journals, the seventh side of leadership has to be there – a serving heart.

These are leaders who understand they are not in a position of authority to dominate people, to crush them, to browbeat them, to maneuver them, to manipulate them, but they're there to serve other people.

And when you as a leader grasp that concept, you move into a very elite group. When you understand the importance of a serving heart, you move into the leadership level of a William Wilberforce, a David Livingstone, an Albert Schweitzer, an Abraham Lincoln, a Mother Teresa, a Nelson Mandela, a Mahatma Gandhi, a John Wooden, a Billy

Graham, a Ronald Reagan, or a Martin Luther King, Jr. When you have a serving heart, that's the league you're in.

I've raised enough children to know that the first piece of equipment you need when a child comes into the world is called a Pamper. You'd better have one ready. Shortly thereafter, the second piece of equipment you'll need handy is a bib.

Embroidered on every bib are these words: "It's all about me." Inevitably, a lot of those children with bibs are going to grow up and become leaders. And, we've certainly seen a good many of them who never take the bib off and they go through a life of leadership with a bib embroidered, "It's all about me." They cry, "Serve *me*, I'm gonna do what pleases *me*; it's all about *me*."

Eventually, one of two things will have to happen. First, the leader must make a decision to take off the bib voluntarily, or, second, the bib will get ripped off non-voluntarily. That can be very traumatic.

When a leader decides to voluntarily take off the bib and replace it with an apron, good things begin to happen. Embroidered on the front of every apron are the words, "Shaped to Serve." When a leader starts wearing the apron, he'll become legendary.

I guarantee you one thing – Coach Bryant wore the apron; he was "Shaped to Serve." Down deep inside that rough, tough exterior was a soft heart, a man of compassion, a servant to his fellow man.

Pat Dye, an assistant coach for Bryant from 1965-73, sums it up best. In Allen Barra's book *The Last Coach*, Dye says, "There are a lot people walking around out there – friends, former players, students who attended college on the scholarship fund he helped set up – people who hit on hard times that don't even know they were helped by him and who he never wanted to know because he thought it might embarrass them."

Linda Knowles, who served as Bryant's secretary his last season, said, "Coach did so much behind the scenes. We had a janitor in the early sixties who was having a tough time. Coach provided him a room in our building to live in, got him a television, and wrote him a monthly check. Coach was a compassionate man.

"One day a father called us from Tennessee to tell Coach his son was dying and his last wish was to meet Coach Bryant. Coach made the trip up there to see the boy, who died two days later. Coach would do those kinds of things regularly."

Jimmy Tom Goostree, son of long-time athletic trainer Jim Goostree, had inside access to Bryant's servant mentality. "There was a compassionate, benevolent side to Coach Bryant," Goostree said. "He helped so many people and no one ever heard about it. Inside that tough outer shell beat a very soft heart."

Julie Strauss McLaughlin, co-producer of *The Bear Bryant Show*, recalls Bryant's routine while in the studio. "Before the show, Coach would call sick kids or people in the hospital," McLaughlin said. "He would say, 'Hello, this is Paul Bryant. They tell me you're not feeling well.' Then you would hear, 'Yes, it's Paul Bryant. It's not a joke.'"

Billy Varner, for many years Coach Bryant's security guard and driver, said, "Coach sure enjoyed helping children. He made a lot of trips to Children's Hospital up in Birmingham to see them. He also made many phone calls and wrote a lot of letters."

Jimmy Sharpe, an Alabama player and assistant coach for Bryant, adds, "People ask me all the time, 'What was Bear like?' They're shocked when I tell them, 'He was a compassionate man.' He was very sensitive and humble and he understood people."

All-American defensive back Jeremiah Castille credits Bryant for steering him into the ministry. "Coach's greatest strength as a leader was his commitment to people, his love for people," said Castille, who served as a pallbearer at Bryant's funeral. "I met him when I was 18 years old when he was recruiting me. Four years later, when I walked away from Coach, I knew I had a father away from home. He just cared about people and especially the little guy.

"I quote Coach every day and think about him all the time. I'm involved in ministry today because of how I saw him serve other people."

On a regular basis, Bryant performed "random acts of kindness" long before such a phrase became popular. Even those closest to him, many of whom felt Bryant's frequent wrath *on* the field, were certainly not excluded from his compassion *off* the field.

"When I was a sophomore at Kentucky, my mother died at age 47," said Neil Lowry, a guard for Bryant from 1952-54. "Coach Bryant brought me to his office to tell me. He knew I had no money to get back to Youngstown, Ohio, so he bought me a ticket to go home. Then he called three times to check up on me. The man was awfully kind to me and to others because he cared for people."

As a paralyzed 10-year old boy on his deathbed, Gary Banister in 1958 experienced first-hand Bryant's compassion in Montgomery's St. Jude's Catholic Hospital. Stricken suddenly with Guillain-Barré syndrome, Banister tasted death once, but was revived in the hospital morgue. After awaking from a 17-day coma, he found himself in an iron lung – a breathing machine invented by a blacksmith – pumping in and out to keep him alive. During his 87-day hospital stay, one particular visitor forever changed his life.

"One day, a large man came into my room," Banister recalls. "I didn't know who he was. He put his hand on top of the iron lung and walked around it three or four times. He put his hands on my emaciated face and said, 'If you ever want to make anything out of yourself, you are going to have to get out of this contraption first.'

"After he walked out, my nurse, who did my talking for me, asked me if I knew who that was. Then she answered for me, 'Well, of course you don't. That was Paul Bryant, head football coach at the University of Alabama.' It was then, after she told me who he was, that I remembered him also saying, 'Get out of that contraption and come play for me.' I have no idea how he knew I was there.

"Skip ahead a few months to May of 1959, at the Elmore County Alumni Meeting in the Tallassee High School cafeteria," Banister continued. "I was now 11 years old, out of the iron lung, but with braces on my hands, legs, back, and neck. I was in a wheelchair, but I could stand and walk slowly.

"Coach Bryant was the speaker and after he finished, he received a standing ovation. Then, he told everyone, 'Please sit down. I'm not through. There's a boy in the audience who's coachable and I want him to come up here.'

"He called my name. I pushed back from the table and several men offered to help. Coach said, 'Leave him alone.' I got to the steps and he said, 'Are you coming, or not?' Slowly, one step at a time, I climbed. I got up there and he said, 'I'm going to sign you today. You're coming to the University of Alabama football team.'"

Even with extensive physical therapy, Banister could play football only through his junior high days. But Bryant, in his own servant-hearted way, never forgot his promise to Banister, allowing him to serve as a student manager from 1967-71. For Banister, it was a life-changing experience.

"Coach Bryant taught me that obstacles could and should be overcome, that handicaps are only a figment of one's imagination," Banister said. "Even though I never caught a pass, gained a yard, made a tackle, or blocked an opponent, Coach Bryant made me feel, with every fiber of my body, that Alabama could not win unless I was there on the sidelines going about my duties as team manager.

"Paul Bryant – the best coach in major college football history and the best friend I have ever had. Without him, there would have been no college education, probably no feeling of self-worth, and definitely no understanding of the value in the statement that 'adversity builds character.'"

Ray Perkins, who succeeded Bryant at Alabama, recalls fondly a time when Bryant came to his rescue. "I sustained a serious head injury and had to have a brain operation during the spring of my freshman year," said Perkins, a 1966 All-American receiver for the Tide. "He came up to Birmingham, got a hotel room, and was in my hospital room every day for nine days.

"That showed me a lot about the man, and gave me a lot of respect for him as a man, not just the coach of the football team."

In February of 1972, Bryant received word that four of his players – Marvin Barron, Rand Lambert, Jeff Rouzie, and Chuck Strickland – had been in a serious accident. Today, almost 40 years later, Barron marvels at Bryant's compassion during that time.

"I had the personal fortune and misfortune to find out how deeply Coach Bryant cared about me as a person as well as a player," Barron said. "In the wreck, we met a very big truck, up close and personal, on a country road.

"Initially, my worst injury was my right leg, which was broken in three places. However, before the night was over, I almost died when an embolism from the breaks went to my lungs. My mother and family were called and told to come immediately, in the belief that I was dying.

"Obviously, I survived, but during my month-long stay in the hospital, Coach Bryant's presence was such a comfort and inspiration to me and to my family. When I was in the intensive care unit, Coach Bryant seemed to be there every time I opened my eyes. I was told that he would just walk right in anytime. No one was brave enough to tell him about visiting hours.

"Although I didn't know it at the time, that wreck would end my playing days. I wanted to play again so badly and prove to Coach Bryant that I had what it takes to come back, so I put everything I had into my rehabilitation. I walked first on my crutches, then with a brace, then with a limp, and finally onto the practice field.

"Although my leg couldn't withstand the rigors of football again, the determination to play again for Coach Bryant gave me the incentive I needed to rehabilitate myself in such a way that I don't have any physical limitations today. For this and so very many other things, I will always be grateful to him.

"Even though I never played again, Coach Bryant saw to it that I finished my degree on scholarship. He also allowed me to be a student coach and later a graduate assistant coach. He never quit caring and helping. I will always cherish the privilege of playing, coaching, and associating with Coach Bryant."

Take a look at Alabama's all-time football lettermen list and you won't find the name of Kent Waldrep. But thanks to Bryant's caring heart, he might as well be on there.

On October 26, 1974, in the Tide's 41-3 win over an out-matched squad from Texas Christian University, tragedy struck when Waldrep, playing running back for the Horned Frogs, scurried around right end and was met by three Tide tacklers. In the mass of four bodies, the three in Crimson jerseys hopped up. A motionless Waldrep lay on the Legion Field turf, a victim of a severe spinal cord injury and a crushed vertebra.

Waldrep was immediately transported to nearby University Hospital, where he had emergency surgery. During Waldrep's month-long hospital stay, Bryant treated him like one of his own.

"Coach Bryant must've been up there three to four days a week," said Waldrep, who remains paralyzed, but has limited use of his arms. "Sometimes, he would come into the room and sometimes he would stay in the hall talking to my mom and dad.

"My parents said there wasn't a time that Coach didn't have a tear in his eye. But in my room, in front of me, he never cried. He was totally uplifting and encouraging. He would put his hand on mine and say, 'When are you going to get up and leave this place?'"

Waldrep did leave Birmingham, but never to walk again. In the ensuing months, Bryant helped raised funds for Waldrep's rehabilitation. Baseball friends George Steinbrenner and Charlie Finley, who had been Bryant's guests at the game in which Waldrep was injured, pitched in to help.

Fittingly, Bryant's generosity to Waldrep more than 35 years ago keeps giving today. "Coach Bryant always told me if I ever had a family, he wanted my children to come to Alabama," said Waldrep, an honorary member of the A-Club, Alabama's letter winners organization. "And, he wanted them to come on the Bryant scholarship, which is normally reserved for children of his former players.

"Thanks to Mal Moore seeing it through, my oldest son Trey just finished Alabama last spring and my youngest son Charley is there now."

To this day, Waldrep's entire family is appreciative of Bryant, who they say went beyond the call of duty. "Coach Bryant and the commitment he demonstrated to me and my family was totally unexpected," said Waldrep, founder of the Kent Waldrep National Paralysis Foundation in Dallas. "They took us in, adopted us, and treated us like one of their own."

I could go on and on about Bryant and his compassionate heart. For every one story you've ever heard, I bet there are a hundred out there that no one even knows about. Hospital visits, get-well phone calls, fundraisers, anonymous gifts for children's charities, autographed photos for devoted fans, secret appointments with the terminally ill, you name it and Bryant did it.

It just makes sense that someone with such a servant heart would have a strong faith in God. After all, it was Jesus Christ who came to earth to *serve*, not to *be served* (Mathew 20:28). Since then, generations of servant-hearted leaders have heeded Jesus' words. Serving others is a basic tenet of Christianity.

We won't attempt a detailed study of Bryant's faith, other than to mention that all evidence points to it being a strong one, especially later in life. Throughout my interviews for this book, there were several mentions of him being a praying man.

Jimmy Smothers, former sports editor of *The Gadsden Times* and a Bryant family friend, says Bryant was "a praying man who acknowledged God both publicly and privately." The late Jim Goostree, Bryant's athletic trainer, once said, "Some of the most tender, thankful, and sincere prayers I've ever heard were prayed in an athletic setting by Paul Bryant."

As well, many players acknowledged Bryant encouraging them to have a strong faith and to make prayer an important part of their lives. Andy Gothard, a defensive back and graduate assistant coach in the mid-1970s, heard Bryant many times say, "We want you to improve in the three areas of life – mentally, spiritually, and physically."

In September 1964, Bryant gave his blessings to the startup of a Fellowship of Christian Athletes chapter on campus. Wayne Atcheson, then a sports information graduate assistant, and eight student-athletes formed what remains today as the nation's longest-running FCA chapter.

Gene Stallings, an assistant coach for Bryant from 1958-64, tells of a call Bryant made to him after Stallings had become head coach at Texas A&M. "One day I received a phone call from Coach Bryant," Stallings fondly recalls. "Coach said, 'Bebes, do you know what is the worst thing that has happened to our football team? It's the FCA. Those players are doing nothing but hugging on one another, loving on one another and they won't hit anybody.'

"After the season, after they had won a national championship, I got another call from Coach Bryant. He said, 'Bebes, do you know what is the best thing that has happened to our football team? It's the FCA. It has brought such a oneness and closeness to our team. We were unified because of the influence FCA had on our team.'"

If anyone had a good pulse on Bryant's faith, it was Grant Teaff, head football coach at Baylor from 1972-92. For years, Teaff has been a spiritual giant in athletic circles and a key supporter of FCA. On the field, Bryant and Teaff faced off twice, with the Tide winning handily each time. Off the field, it was at the annual coaches' conferences that Bryant and Teaff shared a friendship about which few people knew.

"Coach Bryant and I had developed a common bond over the years," said Teaff, currently executive director of the American Football Coaches Association. "At our conventions, he would seek me out and we had some great conversations. Every summer, he would ask me to come to Tuscaloosa to share my faith with his players and staff, as he had them in church on the first Sunday they returned for two-a-days. Even though my team was in two-a-days, he persistently called me for about five years straight, and I always had to turn him down.

"In early January of 1983, Coach Bryant attended our national coaches' convention at the Biltmore Hotel in Los Angeles. After the awards luncheon, I was sitting alone at a table going over my notes for an afternoon presentation I had to make. He came over and sat down next to me with an intense look on his face.

"He said, 'Grant, I want to tell you something. I want to tell you what I'd do differently if I could do it all over again.' I thought, 'Install the wishbone sooner? Run another type defense? Treat his coaches and players differently?'

"Then he said to me, 'Grant, I would let everybody know that I'm a Christian. I am one and I didn't tell them.'

"Three weeks later, Coach Bryant died. I'll never forget my last visit with him."

Teaff's encounter with a transparent and humble Bryant remains a life-long memory. "I think in his own way, Coach Bryant was trying to tell me that his faith, and that of his players, was a top priority for him, although few people in the secular world knew that," Teaff said. "On that special day in California, he evidently wanted me to know for sure that he was a Christian, and that he regretted not letting the world know as well.

"I felt a deep sense of relief that this renowned football coach, who projected many different images to many different individuals, on that day projected to me that we were more than friends.

"We were, in fact, brothers in Christ."

THE AUTHORS ACKNOWLEDGE AND THANK ALL THOSE WHO CONTRIBUTED TO
Bear Bryant on Leadership:

Ernie Accorsi

Mickey Andrews

Leon Ashford

Wayne Atcheson

Buddy Aydelette

Gary Banister

Jimmy Bank

Allen Barra

Marvin Barron

Tim Bates

Bill Battle

Bob Baumhower

Sam Behr

Duffy Boles

Clyde Bolton

Harry Bonk

Paul Boschung

Bobby Bowden

Jim Bowman

Steve Bowman

Byron Braggs

John David Briley

Johnny Brooker

Tommy Brooker

Frank Broyles

Jim Bunch

Neil Callaway

Jeremiah Castille

Rebecca Christian

Mike Clements

Ken Coley

Beano Cook

Paul Crane

Sylvester Croom

John David Crow

John Croyle

Allen Crumbley

Fran Curci

Bill Curry

David Cutcliffe

Bill Davis

Ricky Davis

Tim Davis

Frank Deford

Jim Dent

Doug Dickey

Paul Dietzel

Vince Dooley

Joe Drach

Jerry Duncan

Keith Dunnavant

Ron Durby

Pat Dye

Scooter Dyess

Roy Exum

Paul Finebaum

Danny Ford

Steve Ford

Les Fowler

Jimmy Fuller

Leon Fuller

Rickey Gilliland

Creed Gilmer

Dennis Goehring

Jimmy Tom Goostree

Don Gossett

Andy Gothard

Preston Gothard

Alan Gray

Winston Groom

Clem Gryska

Larry Guest

Mike Hall

David Hannah

Jim Bob Harris

Mickey Herskowitz

Jimmy Hinton

Butch Hobson

Darwin Holt

Lou Holtz

Dennis Homan

Wendell Hudson

Scott Hunter

Cecil Hurt

Keith Jackson

Wilbur Jackson

Bobby Johns

Joey Jones

Wah Wah Jones

Lee Roy Jordan

E.J. Junior

Lou Karibo

Peter Kim

Linda Knowles

Joe Koch

Jim Krapf

Barry Krauss

Charlie Land

K.J. Lazenby

Murray Legg

Walter Lewis

Eddie Lowe

Woodrow Lowe

Neil Lowry

Bill Lumpkin

Marty Lyons

Colin "Big C" MacGuire

Johnny Majors

Jackie Maness

David Mathews

Ray Maxwell

Gaylon McCollough

Tom McEwen

Mike McKenzie

Julie Strauss McLaughlin

David McMakin

Kirk McNair

Don McNeal

Mike McQueen

Steve Meilinger

Ken Meyer

Dewey Mitchell

Dick Mitchell

John Mitchell

Mary Harmon Tyson
Moman

Bud Moore

Mal Moore

Malcolm Moran

Steve Mott

Brent Musburger

Johnny Musso

Joe Namath

Tony Nathan

Billy Neighbors

Wes Neighbors

Benny Nelson

Ozzie Newsome

C.M. Newton

Johnny Nicola

Herschel Nissenson

Lanny Norris

Major Ogilvie

Bill "Brother" Oliver

Tom Osborne

Wayne Owen

Jack Pardee

Babe Parilli

Robin Parkhouse

Ara Parseghian

Jerry Pate

Ray Perkins

Bum Phillips

Billy Pickard

Alan Pizzitola

Edwin Pope

Dee Powell

Jim Proffitt

John Pruett

George Pugh

Keith Pugh

Mike Raines

Pat Raines

Tubby Raymond

Delbert Reed

Billy Richardson

Joe Robbins

Ronny Robertson

Jeff Rouzie

Larry Ruffin

Dick Rushing

Gary Rutledge

Jack Rutledge

Jeff Rutledge

Alvin Samples

James Sanderson

Wimp Sanderson

Kurt Schmissrauter

Howard Schnellenberger

Ed Schwarz

Randy Scott

Jimmy Sharpe

Steadman Shealy

Jackie Sherrill

Bennie Sinclair

Dave Sington

Fred Sington, Jr.

Steve Sloan

Jack Smalley

Barry Smith

Bobby Smith

George Smith

Jimmy Smothers

Steve Sprayberry

Kenny Stabler

Gene Stallings

Dwight Stephenson

Marvin Tate

Grant Teaff

Joab Thomas

Richard Todd

Pat Trammell, Jr.

Mike Tucker

Victor Turyn

Marc Tyson

John Underwood

Billy Varner

Eddie Versprille

Kent Waldrep

Dink Wall

Wayne Wheeler

Darryl White

Gary White

Steve Whitman

Tommy Wilcox

Ken Wilder

Richard Williamson

Rich Wingo

Dexter Wood

Russ Wood

Glenn Woodruff

ACKNOWLEDGMENTS

With deep appreciation we acknowledge the support and guidance of the following people who helped make this book possible:

Special thanks to Alex Martins, Bob Vander Weide and Rich DeVos of the Orlando Magic.

Thanks also to my writing partner Tommy Ford for his superb contributions in shaping this manuscript.

Hats off to four dependable associates—my assistant Latria Graham, my trusted and valuable colleague Andrew Herdliska, my creative consultant Ken Hussar, and my ace typist Fran Thomas.

Hearty thanks also go to my friends at Advantage Media Group. Thank you all for believing that we had something important to share and for providing the support and the forum to say it. Special thanks to founder Adam Witty for your continued support and encouragement.

And finally, special thanks and appreciation go to my wife, Ruth, and my supportive children and grandchildren. They are truly the backbone of my life.

—PAT WILLIAMS

ABOUT THE AUTHORS

PAT WILLIAMS (ORLANDO, FLORIDA) - Few people know leadership better than Orlando Magic co-founder Pat Williams. A sports executive for over 40 years, Williams has led more teams than most of his contemporaries combined. The former General Manager of the Orlando Magic, Philadelphia 76ers, Atlanta Hawks, and Chicago Bulls, Williams is the prolific author of over 10 books on leadership, most recently *Lincoln Speaks to Leaders*. Williams is a highly-acclaimed professional speaker, having keynoted for dozens of Fortune 500 organizations and has appeared on hundreds of news programs including *The Today Show*. Williams and his wife Ruth reside in Orlando and are parents to 19 children (15 adopted from third world countries).

TOMMY FORD (TUSCALOOSA, ALABAMA) - Few people know the University of Alabama and the coaches and former players better than Tommy Ford. Ford knows his Alabama football, having served as sports editor of *The Crimson White* while in school at Alabama. In his professional career, Ford has served the Athletic Department as Ticket Manager, Director of TIDE PRIDE, and currently as Director of Donor Programs. Ford is the author of *Alabama's Family Tides*, a book about families of Alabama football, the *Alabama All-Access Football Vault*, and the *Alabama-Auburn Rivalry Football Vault*.

YOU CAN CONTACT PAT WILLIAMS AT:

Pat Williams

c/o Orlando Magic

8701 Maitland Summit Boulevard

Orlando, FL 32810

(407) 916-2404

pwilliams@orlandomagic.com

Visit Pat Williams' website at:

www.PatWilliamsMotivate.com

If you would like to set up a speaking engagement for Pat Williams, please call Andrew Herdliska at 407-916-2401 or e-mail him at aherdliska@orlandomagic.com.

We would love to hear from you. Please send your comments about this book to Pat Williams at the above address or in care of our publisher at the address below. Thank you.

Adam Witty
Advantage Media Group
192 E Bay Street, Suite 210
Charleston, SC 29401